beside
still
waters

resources for shepherds in the market place

SMYTH&HELWYS
PUBLISHING INCORPORATED MACON, GEORGIA

j. stephen muse | *editor*

Smyth & Helwys Publishing, Inc.
6316 Peake Road
Macon, Georgia 31210-3960
1-800-747-3016
©2000 by Smyth & Helwys Publishing
All rights reserved.
Printed in the United States of America.

J. Stephen Muse

The paper used in this publication meets the minimum requirements of
American National Standard for Information Sciences—Permanence of
Paper for Printed Library Materials.
ANSI Z39.48–1984. (alk. paper)

Unless otherwise indicated, all biblical quotations are taken from the
New Revised Standard Version (NRSV).

Library of Congress Cataloging-in-Publication Data

Muse, J. Stephen
      Beside Still Waters:
      Restoring the Souls of Shepherds in the Marketplace
      p.   cm.
      Includes bibliographical references.
      (alk. paper)
      1. Bible. O.T. Psalms—Liturgical use.
      I. Title.   II. Series.
      BS1435.M38   2000
      223'2.06—dc21   99-38656
                                                              CIP
ISBN 1-57312-317-X

Contents

Preface

Beside *Still Waters* has been a labor of love, conceived in the hearts of pastors working with fellow pastors and written for clergy who need quick medicine for the restoration of their souls and long-term healing. The authors have among themselves more than two hundred years of experience in the ministry of pastoral care and counseling. Many of them currently serve, or have served in the past, on the front lines of the clergy-in-crisis-program at the Pastoral Institute in Columbus, Georgia. Their counsel is practical and immediately useful for all clergy, including those who wish to safeguard the integrity and longevity of their ministry, those who are reaching out for redirection while in the midst of many demands and obligations, and those who simply seek to keep afloat. None will be disappointed.

Ministers from all geographic regions and from every denomination are subject to the same stresses and problems that plague all people, but theirs is also a unique burden. No other profession has the close emotional involvement with as many people in the intimate and tragic moments of their lives. No other profession subjects individuals to such a wide range of expectations and unconscious projections. Consider all the births, deaths, baptisms, weddings, conflicts, hospitalizations, and family crises that accrue to any given family. Multiply these by the number of families in a given parish. Now add in the personality style, illnesses, marriage and family stresses of the minister's own life and family. You'll find that the sum equals the enormous demands of ministry that leave clergy vulnerable to a variety of "viruses" that attack the sense of pastoral call. If not discovered and treated, these symptoms can ultimately lead to compassion fatigue and burn-out. Ministers who are unable to fulfill the perceived demands of the parish and/or meet their own legitimate human needs at the same time may begin to feel like failures—hopeless, angry, and cut off from God.

Each chapter of this book can stand alone as a resource for clergy having difficulties in that particular area. Or taken together, in the context of the beloved 23rd Psalm, the volume addresses the most critical areas of clergy care that support a long-term ministry: protecting the sense of call to ministry, identifying unconscious motivations that distort priorities, dealing with difficult parishioners, disruptions in clergy family life, prayer and spiritual direction, sabbaticals, maintaining ethical boundaries in intimacy, relocation grief, conflict resolution in the church, and the ministry of preaching.

Each chapter addresses an area that can fatally cripple even the most talented and sincere minister if it is ignored. Personal examples and accounts of ministers and churches in the midst of crisis in these areas are recounted along with helpful statistics, Scripture, resources, and proven suggestions for restoring balance. Also included is an appendix with information on the Pastoral Institute's Turner Clergy Center, which offers a nationwide service of crisis intervention, counseling, education, and support for clergy and their families.

For persons just beginning the pastoral ministry, we hope this volume will serve as a useful roadmap for recognizing dangerous territory before any major breakdown occurs. There is much to learn from those who have found themselves upon rocky shoals. I believe it was the late Henri Nouwen, in his classic volume *The Wounded Healer*, who observed, "You can't expect someone to lead you out of the desert who has never been there." The authors of this volume speak both from their personal experiences and from the experiences of clergy with whom they have counseled through the years.

Several people in addition to the contributors have been gracious enough to give their time and care to this project, and it would not be right that their names go unheard. Tina Smith and Jim Metzger helped shape the manuscript into a form that was acceptable to publishing standards. I appreciate them for their eye for detail and their willingness to help in a time-consuming task that I do not enjoy. I hope your reward will be great in heaven!

Special thanks to Gary McCullough, reference librarian at the Bradley Memorial Public Library in Columbus, Georgia, for helping me track down the full citations for some renegade quotations.

Finally, we dedicate this book to all the men and women who have responded to the Good Shepherd's call. I pray that with the Lord's blessing, this volume may provide hearty nourishment along the way and that you may finish the course that the Holy Spirit has bid you to begin.

Keeping the Wellsprings of Ministry Clear

Stephen Muse, Ph.D.

"The Lord is my shepherd, I shall not want."

Responding to the Good Shepherd's voice is the wellspring of authentic pastoral ministry. What happens when other motivations obscure God's place in the minister's life? Attempting to get the parish to love you, responding to anxious pressure to heal parishioners' wounds while ignoring your own, or trying to carve a personal identity out of your work may be indicators of a contaminated wellspring. This chapter examines how unconscious attempts at self-healing, which result from unfinished business in the minister's family of origin, can muddy the well. It can leave ministers more vulnerable to depression, a sense of failure, fatigue, and burn-out.

"I don't know where it will lead or what God wants. I only know that I want to give my life to God." The man's words were both a statement and a fervent question, spoken with tears of gratitude, sadness, and joy. Quietly his pastor told this man, "It sounds like God is calling you to the ministry." "But I don't know that for sure," he responded. At midlife, contemplating a second career, the man continued, "I don't have a clear sense of what form this should take." "It is not necessary to worry about this. The Holy Spirit will lead when the time is right," the pastor assured.

The yoke of Christ's ministry is experienced in its purest form, as the easiest and lightest of all burdens, not as an imposition upon the soul from without, but as an inspiration from deep within. How this response eventually unfolds is as different and as similar as each person. Whatever mixed motivations may eventually obscure that pure call, one thing can be said with certainty: The sheep hear the Shepherd's voice; other voices they will not heed. The Good Shepherd's voice sounding in the depths of the heart is the source of the call to Christian ministry. Remaining in contact with that voice in the midst of a cacophony of others is the means of sustaining and maintaining priorities through a variety of wilderness experiences inevitable in parish life. The saying is sure, ". . . apart from me you can do nothing" (John 15:5).

Unconscious Dimensions of the "Call" to Ministry

Garrett entered a therapy relationship for chronic depression, which he had been suffering for years since leaving the pastoral ministry. It had grown more oppressive for him following a career move into the counseling field, which had ended in burnout and further disillusionment, damaging his sense of self-worth even more.

An exceptionally bright man with a humble demeanor, Garrett felt hopeless. He had tried psychotherapy previously, but without success. "Nothing has ever helped me. I'm beginning to believe the problem is just me. I've been a failure at everything I've tried in my life."

When I hear expressions such as "always," "never," and "every time," my antennas go up. Few things in this world are so clear-cut as to be *always* and *never* the case (perhaps with the exception of "never say never"). Such words alert me to look for a continuing childhood wound. I suspected that somehow Garrett's sense of "belovedness" was injured. I wondered how this happened and if it might have anything to do with the reason why parish ministry was such a strain for this obviously well-educated, dedicated, sensitive, and capable man.

Garrett suffered from conflict with authority figures. He never felt good enough and had a smoldering resistance inside that he could not quite account for in terms of actual circumstances. Although he would give long hours to sermon preparation and visit all the sick in his parish, he felt that he had not done enough. When he sat with people during visitation, their problems weighed heavily upon him, and he felt inadequate to ease their suffering. He felt he wasn't personable enough and that his sermons were poor. Everything took on an edge of invalidation for him. If he was not already depressed, his way of thinking would certainly do the job quickly enough. Not surprisingly, after a half dozen years in the parish he had become exhausted emotionally and so thoroughly disillusioned that he had quit and entered the field of social work.

He told me that as a boy he had always preferred mathematics and physics and had wanted to be an engineer, but his parents had frowned on that career goal and never encouraged him in it. In exploring life in his family of origin, he spoke of an extramarital affair his father had when Garrett was entering adolescence. The family never discussed it, but he knew about it—and his mother was aware that he knew. The tension increased during his adolescence. He related story after story of sitting at the dinner table in a tension "you could grab hold of with a pair of pliers," while his mother twisted "little barbs" into his father. She did this by way of her comments to Garrett, who usually said nothing, but inwardly shrank away with increased anxiety that eventually became numbness. Nothing was ever said directly, but Garrett knew what his mother was doing, and it began to tear him up inside emotionally and to separate him from his father.

I asked Garrett how he came to experience his call to ministry. The answer he gave helped me begin to make the connection between his childhood wound and the depression that enveloped him in ministry when he found he could not satisfy the demands of the parish. Keep in mind that in our weekly meetings Garrett rarely showed any visible emotion beyond a flat, tired expression that begged for someone to help him—only to be told, "That won't help." His refractory depression in combination with a sense of "Help me, but I'll resist whatever help you offer" was extremely frustrating.

He had eventually escaped the tension of the dinner table by going away to college. A few years later he was having trouble identifying what he was going to do following graduation. Then, during a summer break, he had taken an extended trip out west. He decided "for some reason I don't know why" to visit a local night club, something he had never done before. While sitting at the bar he found himself watching as a young woman with a little baby was being picked up by a man she had just met. "Suddenly I felt something in my heart, a sadness for that woman. I left the bar knowing that I was called to go into the ministry to help people so their lives didn't have to come to that." He enrolled in seminary and finished his degree, but not without periodic doubts about his calling.

I asked him, "Have you ever considered that you entered the ministry to prevent your father from having an affair and to heal your mother's pain? You have carried your sense of helplessness and anxiety about this situation with you from the beginning, and your depression is more about that than it is any sort of actual inadequacy on your part." For the first time in months he showed a startled response and some emotion as he said, "I never thought of that. I never saw that connection before."

It is the moment you hope for in human relationships: A long-lost personal grief emerges Lazarus-like from its unconscious burial, steps into the light of adult understanding, and in a context of empathy, reanimates a part of the heart that had been protectively closed off. Childhood scripts are like hypnotic suggestions that work beneath awareness to keep us stuck in the same place. Tapping the "original pain," as one of my colleagues refers to the core issues underneath addictive behaviors, in the presence of a new insight and an empathic other who is witness to the event helps to challenge the script.

Had this gifted man understood better his unconscious childhood agenda early on, he might have been able to free himself from a great deal of unnecessary suffering in his parish work. Finding the original pain means freeing the present from the tyranny of the past. On the other hand, he might actually have chosen to become an engineer rather than a pastor. Certainly he would have been able to make a clearer choice. Garrett said he was never really comfortable with people. He was far more attracted to logic and mathematical certainties than the fickle and unpredictable habits of human beings. His parish work had become an extension of the dinner-table suffering of his adolescence. Unconsciously he viewed his parishioners as controlling parents whose constant estrangement from one another taxed his ability as a peacemaker. He was stuck in a hopeless stalemate that could not be directly named and thus never directly healed. It locked him into the same no-win emotional climate he had experienced as a boy and set him firmly on the tracks of pastoral burnout. The worse he felt, the harder he worked because his commitment to God was as deep as his love for his parents. Unfortunately, his anxiety and depression were also so deep that he couldn't heal them.

In his book *Clergy Burnout*, Alban Institute researcher Roy Oswald locates the beginning and end of the accelerating clergy burnout cycle on the linchpin of God's call to the ministry, which manifests as a high idealism and commitment to serve human need. Coming from the innermost being and fueled by a sense of connection with the Living God, the call to ministry exerts an enormous pull on the emotions and understanding of clergy, urging them on because "God will never give you a burden you are unable to lift." Consequently, as Oswald observes,

> In my stress and burnout seminars, one in five clergy scores high on the burnout rating scale. Among clergy who have been in their parish for ten years or more, the number doubles. These clergy still perform their pastoral functions with skill and concern, but they have lost their zest and vitality. They have become dull, hollow, and uninteresting, and they know it. The tragedy is that these are probably some of our most dedicated and committed clergy. They are not really dull and uncreative; they have simply given so much of themselves for so long that they are burned out.[1]

Having begun his call with an idealism reaching to the depths of a boy's heart to heal his parents and get the love he needed to become whole, Garrett found himself at the top of the cycle. He entered parish ministry against the odds of his personality temperament, ready to use his immense intelligence, attention to detail, and capacity for dedication and self-abnegating service toward fulfilling his calling. He helped others "in order not to make them angry" and so that "their feelings wouldn't be hurt," thus simulating what he had learned at the dinner table with his parents. To be an effective pastor, Garrett needed to be free *not* to help. Then he could be present with suffering persons without the pressure of a quick fix. This position is part of what it means to allow God to be God and the minister to be human.

It is vital that ministers be able to disagree with members of their congregation without going into a depression or an anxiety frenzy trying to avoid their anger. At the other extreme is the danger of always seeking approval and warmth from persons at the expense of working through differences of opinion that have nothing to do with whether or not the minister is liked. In the parish ministry, as in therapy, it is critical to have a clear handle on one's own unconscious agendas so as to be able to see others clearly as fully unique and distinct from oneself.

There is, of course, no spiritual value in codependent behavior. Even a quick romp through the Gospels shows scene after scene in which the apostles share memories of Jesus revealing the unmentionables, confronting the places the Pharisees try to hide, and tenderly caring for those who have had nothing but condemnation all their lives. That kind of flexibility and discernment about what others need came from having his eyes open, not only to others, but also to his own unconscious agendas and being in touch with the sources of his personal grief.

Avoiding clergy burnout is difficult enough for healthy personalities who have a clear agenda and capacity for assertiveness, a consistent Sabbath observance, family, friends, and hobbies. But when these elements are missing and a person also suffers from unconscious compulsive motivations, as in Garrett's case, the road to burnout becomes a high-speed railway.

Surrounded by a congregation whose healing is a desperate concern of the minister and whose love the minister desperately needs to heal a childhood wound, physical and emotional exhaustion comes quickly. With repetition, hopelessness and despair and loss of self-esteem are not far behind. Resentment and cynicism replace flagging enthusiasm for ministry and can eventually lead to an apparent loss of faith. The cycle is like a buzz saw chipping away at the minister's sense of self-worth, which in most cases is intimately tied up in the sense of call. As one pastor said, "If I cannot serve people and fulfill my call, I don't want to live." As Oswald points out, the shame and guilt that begin to accumulate and distort the minister's perception are characteristic of addictive cycles. The burning-out clergyperson remembers the poignancy of the call to ministry and resolves to try harder only to repeat the cycle with even more intensity. Repeated attempts of rededication to the call are simply new attempts at controlling an impossible situation. Obviously, identifying unrealistic expectations whose roots stem from unconscious childhood agendas can go a long way toward protecting both minister and parish from this destructive cycle and making room for effective ministry.

The Role of Discernment

Immediately following confirmation of his own call at the time of his baptism in the Jordan River, our Lord was led by the spirit into the solitude of the wilderness where he fasted and prayed for forty days. Presumably he felt the need for discernment following the heartrending revelation from heaven of his belovedness to God. Therefore, he deliberately pulled back from activity even to the extent of seclusion and bodily fasting. One might question his behavior after an experience of hearing God's voice from the heavens. Would not a period of celebration have been more in order?

From earliest beginnings of the church, the period immediately following "peak experiences" of conversion and call to ministry has been identified as a critical time. Without watchfulness it is easy to be led astray by the intense emotional and intellectual echoes that follow such a powerful experience. A usurper may appear inside, posturing and preening and looking in the mirror of the ego, swelling with idealistic pride or vanity and a host of other more subtle passions like fly paper that capture the attention. When these go unnoticed, the result gives truth to the saying "Pride goeth before a fall."

Jesus was intentional about avoiding this dilemma. He frequently took time for prayer and discernment to reprioritize and remain in touch with the source of his ministry—the voice of God. This helped him set limits and avoid fruitless expenditure of energy in places that would fail to achieve God's purposes. Instead of healing all the physical maladies of the sick who had come to him for help in the midst of a sea of human need, he withdrew apart for prayer. When his purpose became clear, he went to other towns to preach repentance as a response to the Kingdom of God that was dawning, "for that is what I came out to do" (Mark 1:38).

To avoid useless or destructive detours in parish work, every minister who would follow our Lord's example must strive to be alert to inevitable demands, both conscious and unconscious, that present themselves along the way. The foundations of such discernment have to do with clarity concerning the motivations for one's call to ministry and with identifying and maintaining priorities that arise from it, particularly as circumstances change and pressures of parish ministry take on different shapes according to the times and seasons.

Motivations for Ministry

In his counsel to one of his many spiritual children, Thomas Merton wrote of the temptation to allow the call to ministry to become entangled with one's personal ego satisfaction—when "God" and "I" become confused. This mistake, if it can be avoided, can go a long way toward preventing eventual burnout.

> The big results are not in your hands or mine, but they suddenly happen, and we can share in them. But there is no point in building our lives on this personal satisfaction, which may be denied us and which after all is not important.
>
> The next step in this process is for you to see that your own thinking about what you are doing is crucially important. You are probably striving to build yourself an identity in your work, out of your work and your witness. You are using it so to speak, to protect yourself against nothingness, annihilation. This is not the right use of your work. All the good that you will do will come not from you but from the fact that you have allowed yourself, in the obedience of faith, to be used by God's love. Think of this yourself, and you can be more open to the power that will work through you without your knowing it.
>
> The real hope, then, is not in something we think we can do but in God who is making something good out of it in some way we cannot see. If you can do God's will, we will be helping in this process, but we will not necessarily know about it beforehand.[2]

Even when the sense of call is clear and deep, Merton's advice is hard to put into practice on a daily basis. It becomes near to impossible when there is a significant amount of unconscious baggage that muddies the wellspring of one's motivations. For example, is the call to ministry a willingness to give of oneself to others as a free gift of love out of a fullness of a sense of self? Or is it more of an attempt to use ministry to achieve a sense of self?

Psychologist Jack Engler researched why poorly integrated persons were attracted to the self-abnegating aspects of mysticism. In distinguishing unhealthy pseudomysticism from the real thing, Engler coined a pithy saying that goes straight to the heart of the difference: "You have to be somebody before you can be nobody."[3] Otherwise, self-denial becomes a kind of developmental arrest that justifies poorly integrated persons who never develop the full sense of assertiveness and self-worth that is necessary for mature self-giving love.

Persons who have not been loved cannot love others. Belovedness provides the most essential ingredient for healthy psychological development, which in turn leads to compassion and conscience. When parents have not sufficiently bestowed on a child the grace of belovedness, that child's adult life can become a feverish attempt to compensate for it. In the case of ministers, the child-parent relationship is recreated and projected in idealized form onto God and onto the relationship with the parish itself, which is then experienced as a continuation of the childhood attempt to find the belovedness that was missing. As one bishop put it, he finds it necessary to ask of his candidates for the priesthood: "Is this a whole person seeking to express his wholeness through the ministry, or is this a person trying to find his wholeness in the ministry?"[4] Variations on this theme are legion. Keep in mind, the problem is not so much that persons entering ministry are wounded, but that they often do not know or attempt to avoid knowing the extent of the injury and how it can affect them in ministry.

Uncovering the Psychic Graffiti

Like Alice in wonderland and other adventurers, when Dorothy first visited the great city of Oz, she was in a land as far away from Kansas as our unconscious mind is from our conscious mind. There she discovered that a different set of laws prevailed than those with which she was familiar. For one, the inhabitants of Oz described their majestic city as the "Emerald City" because of the shimmering green glow cast by the precious stones of its architecture. Dorothy quickly discovered that the city was not what it appeared to be because the green was actually not in the city itself, but in the lenses of the glasses she was wearing.

Each of us view ourselves, others, and the world through a set of lenses. Like Dorothy's green glasses, these lenses change from time to time according to circumstance and other triggers, often without our realizing it. They come in a variety of shapes like the distorted mirrors of a fun house that cause us to appear tall and skinny or short and stocky. They are based on how we experienced the people whom we loved and needed most early in our lives. There are lenses for how we experienced them and lenses for how we experienced them seeing us. There is also a set of feeling tones that link these lenses. Thus when we are relating to others, particularly those in authority, we are likely to view them unconsciously, through our own particular lenses with our own particular set of psychic graffiti. I say graffiti because, like the mirrors at the carnival, none of the lenses are exactly accurate. Compiled of thousands of snapshots placed on top of each other and forming several main perceptions, each lens is as unique as our individual experiences, yet all bear similar sorts of universal themes just like ordinary graffiti that tell the story of their authors. As our Lord counseled, we need to get to know this psychic graffiti or "log" in our own eyes very well so that we will be able to see the "splinter" in our neighbor's more clearly. More often than not, the famous "log and splinter" have come to rest in the homiletical stream of consciousness in the form of a kind of pithy moralism. The meaning is generally taken as something like, "You should practice what you preach" or "The next time you point the finger, look and see that three fingers are pointing back at you." While these statements may be helpful as pneumonic devices on which to hang a Sunday morning exhortation, they miss the depth and richness of Jesus' insight. Countless voices in Christian tradition have returned to this theme that has been echoed through the centuries. Kontzevitch summarizes the patriotic consensus:

> The way to God leads through knowledge of oneself. "No one can know God without knowing himself," repeats St. Athanasius the Great after St. Anthony the Great. . . . Usually people suffer from blindness and self-delusion and are unable to see their fallen state. Therefore, becoming aware of one's own true state and of evil within oneself is the first step toward knowledge of oneself.[5]

Such knowledge of one's unconscious motivations is essential for effective ministry and longevity in the parish. Jesus was able to respond to people's yearnings and sufferings because he had taken his own advice. He knew how the human mind and heart worked because he was intimately acquainted with the depths of his own human nature. Unlike many of his contemporaries, such as the Pharisees who basked in the fickle light of public opinion, Jesus needed no one's praise and adoration to underwrite any kind of public persona to substitute for rootedness in his own particular essence and vocation—not that this was not tempting.

During his wilderness experience it had occurred to Jesus several times to do otherwise. He might take the path of meeting everyone's physical needs. He could, in effect, turn stones into bread to satisfy the appetites of himself and others. In other words, he could have become codependent. He could have run around seeking to give instant gratification to all those who sought him for help. He could have offered them lesser satisfactions than salvation. The long-term results of such an endeavor is disastrous not only for those who receive the bread, but also for the one who would try to give it—to gain even the whole world, and yet lose the one thing that makes it valuable.

Jesus could have jumped off the pinnacle of the temple as an encore, thereby completing his mission quickly by calling attention to himself with supernatural feats, parading around like some kind of super-guru to whip up the praise (and the offerings) of his devotees. Instead, he chose to be himself, leaving the power and the glory of his ministry to God. He would not tempt God. Nevertheless, it almost happened in spite of his choice in Jerusalem at the Passover feast. Many people were dazzled by the signs he did and wanted to make him their superstar on the spot. Realizing this, he did not trust himself to them. Presumably he was able to do this because he was in touch with the resonance that such adoration created in himself. He was intimately familiar with his own ego and its predilections. This hard-won familiarity with the varied terrain of one's inner state helps make acts of discernment possible, and every one of them is a study in the anatomy of the psychic graffiti that psychotherapists call "countertransference."

Unlike many of Jesus' contemporaries who seemed more concerned with keeping up appearances than with observing the contradictions and surprises within themselves and making confession, Jesus knew and lived from the personal and existential depths of his own human existence. He was well aware of the agonies and ecstasies of his life and would no doubt appreciate what the late psychiatrist Harry Stack Sullivan used to say, "We are all more human than anything else." Because he had taken note of his own tendencies during the wilderness testings, Jesus could be merciful toward the weaknesses and limitations of others.

Likewise, in the parish it is necessary to have a clear sense of the sorts of unconscious lenses that are operating in our lives. This is one way of keeping our sense of call clear and pure. When the parish begins to take on the "green" of our own psychic graffiti, it is time to examine our glasses! Just as parishioners can project their unfinished business onto ministers, the same thing can happen in the reverse. Ministers do well to treat themselves to continuing education through personal psychotherapy and spiritual direction to become familiar with their unconscious triggers and to sort out their psychic graffiti enough to have a handle on the kinds of countertransference that are operating in pastoral work.

Wounded Healers or Wounded Stealers?

Before we can properly serve others, we must honestly identify the motivations of our call to ministry, which require us to acknowledge the unfinished business we bring from childhood. Much of the pressure to "succeed" in the parish by means of getting approval and validation from one's parishioners is a result of lack of awareness in this arena.

When the parish takes the place of father and/or mother in the minister's unconscious life—as it did for Garrett—the patterns of relationship that were present in childhood tend to reproduce themselves in the relationship between the minister and the parishioners, just as they do between spouses in a marriage. This can be for blessing or bane, depending on one's orientation to it. All of us are wounded. The question is whether we will be wounded healers[6] or wounded stealers. Self-awareness is a key ingredient in determining the difference.

It is a well-known fact that those who enter the so-called "helping professions," particularly ministry and psychotherapy, often bear significant wounds from their families of origin.[7] To young children at the age of four or five, taking the blame for adult problems is standard operating procedure. Without the benefit of higher cortical functions of the brain, which are not fully developed until the late teenage years, young children experience themselves as at the center of the universe. Their parents' emotional and physical safety is instinctively experienced as important as their own. The sense of where the parents end and the children begin emotionally is not yet distinct. Thus children will sacrifice their own emotional lives to help their parents survive. This adaptation occurs in alcoholic families and in families where a parent is depressed, mentally ill, abusive, or absent due to work demands. Children blame themselves as the cause for their parents' suffering or absence. The younger the children are at the time, the more instinctive self-blame is and the less able they are to identify and verbalize it as adults.

Therefore, with children from this type of background who become ministers, there can be an unconscious predisposition to blame themselves inappropriately for the suffering of others and to help ease that suffering—and their own. These ministers need the parishioners to feel better in the same way that they needed a parent to feel better to avoid the feeling of being bad or to avoid the anxiety associated with fear of abandonment.

There is an important difference between helping others out of God-directed, self-differentiated, compassionate love and helping them out of personal need. Empathy that is the result of my own anxiety is not the same as empathy that is a result of caring for others because they want and need it. It is crucial that ministers be able to bear the burdens of others without wanting their help. Ministers should not have to be at the center of the lives of their parishioners the way that young children need to be the center of their parents' lives. God needs to be the center of all our lives. There is great freedom in this, and it is a freedom that is essential for healthy ministry.

The Value of Woundedness

When recognized and owned by the minister rather than projected onto others, woundedness can be part of the authentic motivations for ministry and can become a means of understanding and compassion for others. But when unrecognized, it becomes a barrier to love and effective ministry as ministers unconsciously seek to heal their woundedness by compulsively interfering with or ignoring what they perceive as similar wounds in others. This in turn can become a façade upheld by religious language that further camouflages the problem and distorts the gospel for others so that both minister and parish suffer accordingly. Thomas Maeder observes,

> One type of clergyman, like one type of psychotherapist, is a repentant sinner who has recognized his or her weakness and can therefore align himself with other mortals in the search for salvation. Another kind, the sealed-off sinner in his most extreme form, is the rigid and damning preacher who exhorts and chastises his flock from above, who has no sympathy for their weaknesses, and who may hurt his congregants by condemning their transgressions, instead of helping by leading them, through understanding, to righteousness. These preachers are so deeply beset by uncertainty and unresolved problems that they have organized their external life through sheer brute force and imposture, but they have left their internal life untouched. They cannot understand their congregants because they cannot understand themselves, and they cannot constructively help with many emotional problems because the solution they have adopted themselves is to cap such tensions tightly and hold them unseen.[8]

Most psychotherapists would not consider doing therapy without getting supervision and personal therapy to protect clients from such unconscious agendas. Clergy cannot afford to do less. As one of the last generalist professions, ministers function as counselors, preachers, social organizers, spiritual directors, administrators, parents, and even entertainers. The minister's place in people's lives is much too important to neglect the kind of self-inquiry that can protect both clergy and the parish from unintended and unnecessary suffering.

If, as Nouwen has suggested, the minister's job is to "help people suffer for the right reasons," certainly it is necessary to do the same for oneself. It is therefore wise for ministers, preferably early on, to look systematically at personal woundedness with an empathic person who is not "needy," but objective and compassionate. The goal is to keep the motivations of the pastoral calling free of the ordinary psychic debris, thereby enabling the minister to continue to hear and obey the Shepherd's still small voice.

Both minister and parishioner benefit from the minister's self-awareness, just as both are injured by the lack of it. It is clear from the Gospels that Jesus knew where to draw limits in his life. Still, many clergy do not believe this is a Christian thing to do. Consequently, they do not draw limits; they continue "helping" until they burn out, not unlike someone suffering the manic phase of a bipolar illness who goes without sufficient sleep for days until the inevitable crash of depression comes. Both the manic patient and the "inspired and dedicated" minister who does not practice legitimate self-care eventually suffer the same fate. For the person with bipolar illness, the cause is largely bio-chemical; whereas for the minister, the roots of the illness are countertransference at the unconscious level. Countertransference that is not recognized is eventually acted out. It can and ought to be one of the minister's best friends in ministry, just as it has become the ally of every mature therapist.

Occasionally clergy may use "spirituality" as a cover for lack of awareness of unconscious motivations. Lack of assertiveness is con-fused with self-denial or repression of anger if it passes as kindness. (This is tantamount to saying that being able to keep my hand on the stove past the point of burning because I don't have any nerves in my hands is a valuable ability.) Lack of assertiveness is not a trait to be admired; rather, it is a pathological condition. Similarly, lack of self-awareness and codependency in parish work are not "carrying one's cross." Useless, avoidable suffering damages both minister and parish-ioner, whereas the necessary suffering of carrying one's cross is part of healthy self-denial that leads to discernment and blesses both minister and parishioner.

Using Psychology Without Making It a Religion

"Nothing could happen then that can't happen now." His words were heavy with rationalism and the weight of disappointed idealism. The voice and physical presence of the minister sitting across from me was tired, and his words were a bitter condensation of the juices of a ministry severed from the root. Perhaps they were quiet, desperate words spoken with a cynical hope of tempting God to prove otherwise. Like the coals of a once-roaring bonfire, the remnants of this man's call to Christian ministry smoldered faintly underneath the damp leaves of ministerial burnout. He was depressed and fighting off a sense of failure and disappointment.

15

By the time I met with him, he was in the process of patching up a one-man dingy to make it through the rising flood of anguish that accompanies such disillusionment in the parish ministry. Using Jungian psychology as his rudder, Christianity had been reduced to a mere symbol of the way to organize the psychic stuff of life on the road to psychological health according to prevailing secular norms. In his mind, anything that could not fit into empirical science and rational philosophical-psychological categories was not applicable. In his case, psychology was serving as a kind of Trojan horse emptying from its entrails an anthropology, an epistemology, and a view of the universe that, taken in sum, amounted to a competing religion itself, though in Christian disguise.

I wondered with this man where his emerging views and the way of Christ diverged. Perhaps he should identify himself as a reformer if he insisted on his current path, but not present himself as a traditional Christian minister. Part of his pain was that he was preaching a "gospel of psychological individuation," and people were not responding. The disparity between the "gospel" he was preaching and the gospel believed "always and by all" since the beginning was taking its toll.

It is one thing to use psychotherapy legitimately to help ferret out the myriad ways of misunderstanding or resisting the Shepherd's voice. It is quite another to lose it amid the chorus of voices from the contemporary secular religion of "evolutionary scientism" or "psychologism." Abandoning rather than deepening their theological moorings, some clergy have uncritically embraced the developmental norms and values inherent in the psychotherapeutic disciplines as substitutes for prayer and obedience to God. This is a dangerous detour that takes persons right back into the messiah trap with God being replaced by "I." Fascinated with "what works" and what "seems reasonable" in the face of the trials and temptation of parish ministry, a psychologized Christianity fits with the task-oriented "I'm in control" mentality of modern secular life. This is a dead end. Self-awareness apart from awareness of God and self-actualization apart from obedience to God is an illusion.

In conjunction with prayer, worship, and study of the Scriptures that support the effort to be obedient to God, good psychotherapy can help keep the well clear of unconscious distortions so that the Shepherd's voice can continue to ring clearly in the heart. Remaining in touch with the water that springs up from this eternal life is the only motivation for pastoral ministry that can sustain a person for the duration. Anything less is simply more of what everyone else is already trying to do, and the church surely has more to offer than that. A "modern St. Anthony," who traded his successful pharmacy holdings for the desert, observes:

> There is no intellectual means of entering into the Gospel, for the Gospel is spiritual. It must be obeyed and lived through the Spirit before it can be understood. If anyone living outside the Gospel tries to understand it he will stumble and fall, and if he dares to try to teach it, he will be a stumbling block to those who follow him. But if anyone has true zeal, burning love, and a total obedience to God and carries out just one of the commandments of the Gospel precisely, that person enters into the mystery of the Gospel without being aware of it.
>
> A sincere and humble acceptance of obedience to God that springs from a heart undefiled by falsehood, hypocrisy, love of display, or exhibitionism, and not looking for any particular results, may be considered the beginning of the true way to the knowledge of God.[9]

In the third century following the Christianization of the Roman Empire under Emperor Constantine, the original St. Anthony of the desert, founder of Christian monasticism, spoke of the goal of the spiritual life in terms of "becoming yourself"—to strip away all pretense and to be genuine. Perfect obedience and perfect simplicity are two sides of the same coin. Answering the call to ministry can be a part of that becoming, provided one's priorities are straight and one's motivations are clear. Ministers who try to be all things to all people will surely lose themselves in the process, and ministry will lose its integrity. "Rev. Smith agrees with whomever he's talking to at the moment," the parishioner complained. "He's two-faced." Actually, ministers can become multiple-faced as they attempt to meet the demands of all the parish and to avoid criticism. In the myriad of faces of parish life, there is only one face to be concerned with—the face of the Good Shepherd in whom we recognize the Living God. As Pope Paul VI put it in Vatican Council II, "If we can remember that behind the face of every person we can find the face of Christ and that in the face of Christ we recognize the face of the heavenly Father, then our humanism becomes Christianity."

If, however, we look to Christ and see only an image of our own human psychology, seeking to find refreshment and orientation to pastoral ministry through man-made tools without the power of the Holy Spirit and the benefit of a revealed theology, we will find the well of life dry and our spirits parched. Like Jesus in the wilderness, the suggestion that we substitute trying to please anyone other than God for any reason other than the Truth is a moment of temptation that recurs often. We are asked to make bread of something other than the Word of God and lead persons to God by means other than the "Way, the Truth, and the Life." To this we must say no, however difficult it may be, and pray with the Apostle that "I can do all things through [Christ] who strengthens me" (Phil 4:13). It is then, in our weakness, that the power and might of God will be most evident and our ministry most effective.

After all, it was in the presence of the memory of this point of brokenness and the response of forgiving grace that our Lord commissioned the apostle Peter to the pastoral work of feeding his lambs. By asking him three times if he loved him, Jesus reminded Peter of the time of his worst failure, when he had denied even knowing the Lord three times. Like King David in Psalm 51, Peter knew well the lesson: "a broken and contrite heart, O God, you will not despise" (v. 17b). This is the psalm that every Orthodox priest in the ancient Divine Liturgy of St. John Chrysostom prays just before beginning preparation for the feeding the flock with the body and blood of Christ. There can be no better preparation for ministry or means of effectively safeguarding it than to return to this point time and again. It is out of the soil of humility born of painful recognition that we are not God, that we cannot do what is asked of us in our call to ministry except by the power of the Holy Spirit at work in us, that the living power of God emerges with renewed force to feed a hungry world. In this sense, the burning-out minister should not despair, but turn to God in prayer and seek help in receiving the gift of renewal that such recognition brings.

Notes

[1]R. Oswald, *Clergy Self-Care: Finding a Balance for Effective Ministry* (New York: Alban Institute Publication, 1991) 67.

[2]W. H. Shannon, *The Hidden Ground of Love: The Letters of Thomas Merton and Religious Experience and Social Concerns* (New York: Farrer, Straus, and Giroux, 1985) 294-97.

[3]J. Engler, "Therapeutic Aims in Psychotherapy and Meditation: Developmental Stages in the Representation of Self," in vol. 16 of *The Journal of Transpersonal Psychology* (1984): 51.

[4]T. Maeder, "Wounded Healers" *The Atlantic Monthly* (January1989): 42.

[5]I. M. Kontzevitch, trans. Olga Koshansky, *The Acquisition of the Holy Spirit in Ancient Russia* (California: St. Herman of Alaska Brotherhood, 1988) 35.

[6]Cf. H. Nouwen, *The Wounded Healer* (New York: Doubleday & Co., 1972).

[7]Maeder, 37-47.

[8]Ibid., 41.

[9]Matthew the Poor, *The Communion of Love* (New York: St. Vladimir's Seminary Press, 1984) 20-21.

Suggested Readings

Jones, Alan. *Soul Making: The Desert Way of Spirituality.* San Francisco: Harper & Row Publishers, 1985. Psychology of the desert fathers for contemporary ears. Wise counsel for clergy who seek to enter more deeply into the life and mystery of Christian faith.

Nouwen, Henri. *In the Name of Jesus.* New York: Crossroad, 1979. A small volume that speaks powerfully about how pastoral vulnerability and humility are the foundations of authentic ministry.

Oswald, Roy. *Clergy Self-Care.* New York: Alban Institute, 1991. An accurate picture of the common factors that weaken the parish ministry and practical helps for dealing with the problem.

Peck, M. Scott. *The Road Less Traveled: A New Psychology of Love, Traditional Values, and Spiritual Growth.* New York: Simon & Schuster, 1978. A synthesis of psychology and traditional spiritual values. Very useful, provided one does not treat Christian formation and psychological maturation as synonymous.

Peterson, E. H. *Working the Angles: The Shape of Pastoral Integrity.* Grand Rapids: Eerdmans, 1987. A clarion call to reorient one's pastoral ministry to the classical calling of prayer, Scripture, and spiritual direction. Challenges the model of Christian ministry that is a sell-out to sociology, success, and the American dream.

Wicks, R. J. *Christian Introspection: Self-Ministry Through Self-Understanding.* New York: Crossroad, 1986. A self-evaluative instrument on the motivations for ministry and Christian life.

Care for the Caregivers

Stephen Muse, Ph.D.

"He makes me lie down in green pastures."

No one can love who has not first been loved. Care for others proceeds from allowing oneself to be cared for. Ministers who do not honor their own legitimate needs for peer relationships, dependency on others, and time for relaxation and renewal are placing themselves, their families, and their ministry in jeopardy. This chapter looks at the necessity for Sabbath and provides examples of ways to care for the caregivers.

Beneath the more obvious expectations that congregations have of their ministers are those that they read in the Gospels. Real pastors "heal the sick, raise the dead, preach the Kingdom of God, and take no money for their labors." Real pastors speak by the Holy Spirit. Real pastors preach with words of power, and their prayers make a difference.

The Gospels record an experience and a vision of life that remain the fervent hope in the hearts of clergy and their congregations. If we respond authentically, Christian faith invites us into a fully human life where human limits are surpassed by the power of God. Without reliance on God, the call of the gospel becomes an impossible expectation that leads into a spiritual desert where the living waters of renewal are scarce and the mirages of lesser destinations evoke unbearable thirst. The road to Jerusalem is littered with the flights and crashes of would-be messiahs and superstars who, like Icarus, have soared too close to the sun on artificial wings. In their plummets back to earth they have frequently taken with them a portion of the Good Shepherd's flock. Such exploits were recognized by the desert fathers who said, "If you see a young man climbing up to heaven on his own power, yank him down. It will be good for him."

In our better moments we know that the power of God is manifest most clearly in our confrontation with the barriers to becoming gods ourselves: "God's power is made perfect in human weakness" (1 Cor 1:26ff). The encounter with limits circumscribed by our own mortality, embedded in creation like a microbe awash in a great ocean, presents both a danger and an opportunity. We can struggle to obey God and walk in faith toward "things unseen," or we can live as if the limits of death and life are one and the same. The ongoing struggle to live by the commandment of love and the continual confessing relationship before an unseen God is not a journey to be taken for any reason other than its own intrinsic value. Truth and life are one. Serious problems arise when the things clergy say and believe diverges too much from what they seek to live.

"Succeeding" in the Ministry

These same superhuman expectations, held aloft by idealism and ignorance of unconscious motivations, leave clergy open to a loss of direction underwritten by the disease of workaholism. As authentic spiritual and theological moorings are severed, ministers can become involved in a kind of "busyness" that gives the appearance of "success" in worldly terms without actually leading to a maturing of personal faith and responsibility for the parish s/he leads. Eugene H. Peterson, who is a veteran of thirty-five years of parish ministry, biblical scholar, and widely respected "pastor of pastors," observes:

> American pastors are abandoning their posts, left and right, and at an alarming rate . . . They have gone whoring after other gods. What they do with their time under the guise of pastoral ministry hasn't the remotest connection with what the church's pastors have done for most of twenty centuries . . . They are preoccupied with shopkeeper's concerns—how to keep the customers happy, how to lure customers away from competitors down the street, how to package the goods so that customer will lay out more money . . .
>
> Great crowds of people have entered into a grand conspiracy to eliminate prayer, Scripture, and spiritual direction from our lives.

They are concerned with our image and standing, with what they can measure, with what produces successful church building programs and impressive attendance charts, with sociological impact and economic viability. They do their best to fill our schedules with meetings and appointments so that there is time for neither solitude nor leisure to be before God, to ponder Scripture, to be unhurried with another person.[1]

© Mary Chambers 1983. Used by Permission.

In the midst of the blaze of activity that takes place in becoming (or remaining) the "successful" church, clergy can easily begin to think in terms of meeting the congregation's worldly demands rather than being faithful to their calling. After a few years they may begin to feel overwhelmed by their task as entertaining and inspiring weekly orators. One Baptist minister, tired after a long and fruitful ministry, remarked wistfully, "The pressure to top last week's sermon is enormous. Baptists will forgive the preacher anything, but a bad sermon will do you in." Add to this expectations of clergy as spiritual guide, marriage counselor, social director, administrative supervisor of staff, political commentator, officiator at baptisms and weddings and funerals, crisis-intervener, and fund-raiser, and you have the ingredients for the role of clergy super-hero. Ministers simply cannot neglect their own health and spiritual life if they are going to be shepherds of the lives of others. "Physician heal thyself" is sage advice and absolutely critical for modern clergy who are in constant danger of succumbing to secular visions of success.

Gaining Success But Losing Integrity

Brad, a talented young minister with a decade of solo experience in the parish and a strong contemplative bent, was invited to consider a job as associate pastor of a large, active multicultural church in a metropolitan area. There were already several ministers on staff, including the senior pastor who was a nationally known preacher. The church had a dazzling array of progressive social programs and outreach ministries. In looking over the materials sent to him by the search committee, Brad noticed that the church lacked a contemplative dimension and the search committee was interested in him in part because they shared a similar perception. Subsequent interviews with the senior minister on a couple of occasions, however, elicited comments from him about prayer as "navel gazing."[2] Brad observed,

> The first time I spoke with him he told me that he "worked seventy to eighty hours a week and expected to go home and drop into bed exhausted, wearing myself out in the cause of Christ. That is what ministry is." Leaving the interview, I felt a little diminished because I had said to him in our first meeting that I wanted to limit my work week to an average of fifty hours in order to protect my marriage and family life. I told him I felt this was important to model for the parish as well. How can I expect others to protect their families and be intentional about keeping contemplative space in their lives if I do not model this with my own life?

The church was in a fine community, and the search committee members were deeply committed people with whom Brad would have enjoyed working, so it was with some regret that he ultimately chose not to pursue the position. The sad fact of the matter is that this particular senior minister, like so many others in similar situations, was a very talented, devoted, and capable leader with tremendous potential. By outward standards, his church was highly visible and successful on several fronts, but the minister had failed to nourish his own soul in the process of leading the congregation. Not long afterwards, Brad learned that the church was on the verge of splitting over the pastor's marital problems and infidelities that had come to light. He divorced and subsequently married his lover—after receiving a large severance package to get him to resign from his position and avoid further scandal.

The limitless demands and egoistic rewards of parish ministry can wear down and eventually divert the energies of even the healthiest and most conscientious of God's servants. Fifty percent of clergy say they cannot meet the demands of the parish.[3] Seventy percent say they have a lower self-image now than when they started the pastorate.[4] This kind of attack on self-esteem presents a danger to clergy who do not intentionally protect their private and spiritual lives sufficiently to get the care and guidance they need for themselves in order to continue caring for others.

When responsibilities weighed down heavily on their shoulders, biblical characters responded in various ways. Abraham pleaded. Moses demanded. Elijah sought a quiet cave. Peter went back to fishing for a time. Even Jesus left people at Peter's doorstep to go into the desert to pray. Why couldn't the senior minister of this thriving congregation see that his pace of life and lack of inner solitude might have something to do with his vulnerability to compromising his priorities and betraying his wife and family? Isolation is a prime ingredient in clergy boundary violations. The ethics committee of the American Association of Pastoral Counselors reports that sexual boundary violations tend to occur most frequently among the best educated and most highly trained clergy who are working in isolation without sufficient accountability.[5]

Keeping the Sabbath Holy and the Mind and Body Whole

Modern medicine is rapidly advancing in its understanding of the interactive nature of mind and body. It appears that the ancient view of the soul being central to the Judeo-Christian perspective and that of modern medicine are converging. For example, endorphins (natural opiates that regulate mood and pain thresholds) are produced at other sites than the brain. Endorphins are manufactured in certain white blood cells and in the gastrointestinal tract, which also has receptor sites for them. Dr. Candace Pert, former chief of brain chemistry at the National Institute of Mental Health (NIMH), has gone on record as saying: "I can no longer make a strong distinction between the brain and the body. Research suggests a need to start thinking about how consciousness can be projected into various parts of the body."[6]

Modern scientific voices speak of the body-mind connections in ways similar to the ancient Hebrews, who did not separate body and soul—as did Westerners following the post-enlightenment perspectives of Descartes. It looks as though what we once thought of as separate entities—body and mind—may be more accurately viewed as "different expressions of the same information carried by chemical transmitters."[7]

This discovery helps to underscore the value and even necessity for observing a Sabbath, which means to "let go and let God." Sabbath is a time to make *being* more important than *doing*; to stand back and let God's handiwork shine in all its glory and goodness. It is not surprising that research has shown that keeping a Sabbath is good for mental health.[8] Numerous studies have confirmed the positive effects of intentional practice of relaxation upon ego formation, emotions, and the body. Inner stillness and the improved quality of attentiveness that are associated with relaxation techniques are prerequisites for the kind of compassion and empathy that underlie intimate relationships. Love and intimacy are good for the spirit *and* the body. Apparently, love not only "bears all things, believes all things, hopes all things, endures all things" (1 Cor 13:7), but it also changes the immune system! Varied examples lend credibility to this theory.

Research involving more than 10,000 subjects studied over a period of five to nine years revealed that "those who were socially isolated had a two- to three-fold increased risk of death from heart disease and from all other causes when compared to those who felt most connected to others. These results were independent of other cardiac risk factors such as cholesterol level, blood pressure, genetics, and so on. Similar results were found in 2,059 subjects from Evans County, Georgia, where the greatest mortality was found in older people with few social ties."[9]

In a Yale University School of Medicine study of 119 men and 40 women undergoing coronary angiography, coronary atherosclerosis significantly decreased for persons who felt loved and supported when compared to those who did not, even after other risk factors had been controlled, including age, sex, income, high blood pressure, serum cholesterol, smoking, diabetes, genetics, and hostility.[10]

Most interestingly of all, researchers discovered that sharing feelings by way of writing in a journal even when no other person was actually present had important physical benefits. At Southern Methodist University in Dallas, Texas, researchers asked a group of students to spend twenty minutes on each of four days writing about a traumatic event in their lives. A control group was asked to spend the same amount of time writing about trivial events. Blood samples taken from both groups before and after this four-day period revealed an increase in immune activity in the self-disclosing group and no change in the control group. Researchers concluded:

> Failure to confide traumatic events is stressful and associated with long-term health problems. Inhibition of thoughts, feelings, or behaviors was associated with physiological work, resulting in increased autonomic nervous system activity. In other words, holding feelings in puts a chronic stress on the heart and on the immune system.[11]

Actuarial tables show that men die ten years earlier than women. In general, men tend to share less about themselves and have a harder time tolerating and disclosing feelings of vulnerability, which research shows could help lengthen our life span. Generally, when persons come to see me for therapy, I ask them whether or not they share their feelings with God and if they feel understood. One young girl struggling with a very painful family situation told me, "I wrote a letter to God at school. I felt a lot better." That one fact told me volumes about this girl's faith and chances of surmounting the obstacles in front of her. The above research lends further credibility to this aspect of prayer.

Dealing with Isolation

Clergy isolated? How can that be? Clergy are surrounded by a sea of human needs and social events. The problem of clergy isolation may seem strange, and yet it is an ever present problem. At a recent clergy seminar 70% of the participants surveyed said they did not have a close friend.[12] Most married clergy claim their spouse is their best source of support, but when clergy are drawn too completely into caregiving for the extended "church family," support at home, often greatly taxed already, can quickly disappear. Research shows that clergy families frequently experience "intrusiveness" from the church family's expectations, which muddy the boundaries of the clergy family.[13] Whose needs come first? "He is married to the church" is a familiar refrain of clergy spouses. The majority of clergy (94%) say they feel pressure to have an "ideal" family, while 80% say their ministries have actually had a negative impact on their families.[14]

Relating to the Church as Extended Family

Psychotherapists who work with families know well the tremendous impact that the parental subsystems can have on married couples. When parents from the couple's respective families of origin do not view their children as separate adults, but as emotional extensions of themselves, numerous problems can arise that interfere with a couple's intimacy. The parents hold unspoken expectations that the couple live as they have lived or raise their children as they have done. These expectations can create tensions between the couple. Overinvolvement with a dependent mother or father who calls "every day without fail" and who "becomes anxious whenever I disagree with her/him" can evoke jealousies and abandonment feelings in the other spouse who feels that the "in-laws" come between them.

When my wife and I were married in the early part of my first pastorate, one of the parishioners who became dear to us and constantly "looked out" for us forewarned me of my extended church family's expectations of their new "clergy couple" that, like father and mother or Aunt Gilda, if not respected, could bode serious repercussions. "It wouldn't be a good idea to have champagne at your reception. *Certain people* would be offended." So we had sparkling cider instead!

Recent research has begun to focus on the unique problems of clergy families, which in effect function as a "subsystem" of the larger church family, replicating the problems of in-laws multiplied by the number of families in the congregation. Subtle but intense pressures resulting from the collective interrelated family systems within the church can scapegoat clergy families. Pastoral counselor R. E. Buxbaum, who regularly consults with congregations, offers an illustration of this phenomena of "scapegoating," regularly seen in marriage and family work, as it occurred in a troubled church with which he worked:

> Ministers can be scapegoated by the system to act out on its behalf. Often in these instances the congregation recreates a common family of origin issue. It can become the means of externalizing an unresolved issue that threatens the well-being of the other people in the system. Consider, for example, the new congregation in which the marriage of three of the first four pastors ended in divorce while serving that congregation. Most of the members of the congregation were couples in their thirties who were highly upwardly mobile and thus highly competitive. A large percentage of couples that were members of this congregation had their own marital problems. They were caught between their own temptations to act out and their pietistic religious convictions. In unconscious, nonverbal ways the congregation system "appointed" their pastors to act out and divorce on their behalf, thereby absolving them of their need to act out and avoiding their feelings of guilt about their own urges. Projecting their own temptations upon the pastors and their spouses, they could take punitive actions toward the pastors and vicariously meet their own unconscious needs for penance and absolution.[15]

Church authorities ignored this psychological interpretation and focused solely on the moral transgression of the pastor, as they had done in past instances, transferring him to a "less-well-paid" appointment as a kind of punishment. Significantly, however, after this interpretation was pointed out to the fifth pastor to serve in this congregation (who subsequently passed along this perspective to the successors), none have had any significant marital problems while serving in this particular congregation.

Family relations of each spouse are frequently the cause of marital problems in couples. For clergy couples, the frequent interruptions created by the life tragedies and events of the larger church family, along with the subtle emotional intrusiveness and unconscious projections and expectations upon clergy families, stretch even the best emotional reserves to the limit. Clergy spouses are particularly vulnerable to the increased demands placed upon them by their circumstances and expectations of the church because, unlike their spouses, they do not have a specific professional role in the church and as a result tend to have fewer coping resources.[16] Among the accumulating stressors for clergy spouses are: increased demands on household labor, frequent relocation, the lack of a "pastor" figure, the assumption that they provide "free labor" in the church, loss of emotional support, and interruption of personal careers.

Frequently these stresses on the couple go unrecognized or minimized because the concerns of the larger church family are "God's work" and must "always" come before "personal concerns" of the minister and his or her family. Men in particular are often reluctant to acknowledge legitimate dependency needs and tend to underestimate the importance of the relational needs of their spouses. Male ministers may talk about vulnerability and intimacy from the pulpit, but their own lives are characterized by denial, workaholism, codependency, competition, and control.

Balancing Between "Burn-Out" and "Rust-Out"

Ministers need to seek an appropriate balance between responding to the demands of their public roles and their personal lives. For a long time little or no attention was given to clergy stress and burnout. Now that the problem is coming to attention, there have been a few instances in which newly trained clergy have been so intent on not burning out that they appear to be in danger of "rusting out." One veteran minister who served on his denomination's board of ministry reported: "We have begun to see clergy who are getting into trouble in their first parishes because they are not responding to the needs of the parish; so zealous are they to protect their private lives." Obviously there must be a balance between the public role and the private self. The gap between the two is like the gap on a spark plug. Being too close or too far away leads to problems in activating activity, and eventually ministry comes to a screeching halt.

Avoiding an Addictive Work Ethic

As in Jesus' day, we cannot serve two masters. Psychiatrist Gerald May points out in his book *Addiction and Grace*[17] that we are either addicts or obedient to God; there is no middle ground. Ministers who would be faithful to their calling cannot afford *not* to be intentional about their interior lives and their accountability to God in prayer. They must grow continually in the awareness of their humanness in healthy ways. Born of the repentance and humility that comes from such awarness, the minister's compassion for others deepens. Being intentional about prayer is a good place to start.[18] This means taking time for contemplation and retreat with God's Word, lest we forfeit our inheritance as human *beings* only to become human *doings*.

Clergy are leaders of the church and, like it or not, many persons choose a congregation based largely on how they respond to the minister. Does he have integrity? Does she "walk her talk?" Very little is gained from ministers who exemplify chronic workaholism and little or no intimacy outside of one-way professional work relationships. Ministers who are burning out (or acting out) are usually assuming too much responsibility for one person. They are trying to answer to everyone but God for everything but the one thing that is most important. To the extent that this occurs, the gospel is compromised and churches become indistinguishable from other civic organizations. Worse, by using Christian language and keeping up appearances, while failing to shepherd sincere souls toward authentic life in Christ, ministers feed the public perception of the church as a place of "hypocrites." One of my clients who regularly attended AA meetings, which he found extremely supportive, said he doesn't attend church anymore because "the people are too scared of really knowing who each other are."

Perhaps we could set the proper tone between parish and minister with an open and honest attitude like this: "Hello my name is Rev. Honest Person, and I am a sinner. Forgive me." In fact, in the Divine Liturgy of the Eastern Orthodox Church the priest turns to the people at several points and bows, asking forgiveness for his unworthiness. More than a mere "ritual," the action is a starting point (and continuing) for effective ministry and a model of Christian human relations. Vulnerability and humility engender themselves in others. Pride and pretense, however, imprison both clergy and parish in an addictive spiral of withdrawal from intimacy to avoid the shame and guilt associated with not being perfect like God. This is tantamount to hitting the parishioners over the head with the club of the Law rather than the summons of grace. It perpetuates the addictive cycle, often inadvertently begun by parents, which creates a pressure within children to succeed to avoid being "unloved." The child's original belovedness is covered by a thick layer of must-becomedness—"If you will only . . . then you will be beloved to me." Without a substantial dose of the medicine of grace to restore a sense of belovedness, the disease is progressive and the soul is slowly starved out. Jungian analyst Marion Woodman observes,

> Addiction to perfection comes in part from the situation in which parents have a concept of what the perfect child would be—perfect athlete, perfect scholar, when 100 percent achievement is the goal. The parents are trapped by this ideal and their whole life is centered around performance. The child then learns how to perform and has an idealized vision of what he or she should be. Anything that doesn't fit in with that ideal has to be pushed back, has to be annihilated, really. As a result, whatever is human in the child, whatever is "dirty"—sexuality, and the plain ordinary world of the body—the child experiences as not part of the perfect idea. Spontaneity—just the natural anger or natural joy even, or the natural love of rocks and mud—is blocked, and the child gets the idea on some level that he or she is unlovable. "Whoever I am in the reality of my being is not lovable," the child concludes.
>
> Natural being is repressed, and performance becomes everything. In any given situation a person subject to this repression will figure out whom to please and then perform in order to please that person, and their own reality is not present in the performance. People begin to live for an ideal—there's nothing else to live for. But if you are living for an ideal, and driving yourself as hard as you can to be perfect—at your job or as a mother or as the perfect wife—you lose

the natural, slow rhythm of life. There's just a rushing, trying to attain the idea. The slower pace of the beat of the earth, the state where you simply *are*, is forgotten.[19]

That "natural slow rhythm of life" is the rhythm of mindfulness, popularly and somewhat sentimentally referred to as "stopping to smell the roses." Brother Lawrence speaks to it in his spiritual classic *The Practice of the Presence of God*. Ministers who live out this discipline will find that those around them receive the message in ways that transcend words. Most of what we imbibe that affects our lives comes not from our preaching, but from our living. As St. Seraphim of Sarov counseled, "Acquire inward peace, and thousands around you will find their salvation." We do not need more sermons, but people who are living words.

Jesus' life remains paradigmatic for Christian ministry. He entered deeply into intimate relationships without codependency, and others were drawn to him—not because of his superhuman vitality, but because of his goodness and humility. He recognized this and invited persons to him on that basis: "Come to me, all you that are weary and carrying heavy burdens, and I will give you rest. Take my yoke upon you, and learn from me; for I am gentle and humble in heart, and you will find rest for your souls" (Matt 11:28). It is clear that Jesus "knew himself" and therefore had an accurate sense for "what is in human beings" and consequently could minister to them without needing them "to testify about anyone" (John 2:25). Jesus took time to be apart, both in a Sabbath and in his emotional needs, even in the face of continuing human suffering all around him. Rather than losing himself while trying to meet each person's immediate needs, Jesus kept his focus on fulfilling God's ultimate purposes in saving all humanity. Modern ministers can afford to do no less

Learning To Suffer for the Right Reasons

There is a difference between taking up your cross and becoming a doormat. It is the minister's job to help persons suffer for the right reasons. This goes for clergy themselves. In addiction counseling we speak of the concept of being an "enabler" of another person's sickness or addiction. Enabling or "codependency" has to do with a useless sort of suffering that the addict's spouse and family members fall into, habitually foregoing their own needs with the intent of "saving" the addict, but in effect only making him/her worse and losing oneself in the process. Ministers need to recognize the difference between the necessary and intentional voluntary suffering of Christian discipline that leads to life and the unnecessary, involuntary suffering that is a mark of psychological ignorance, codependency, passions, and mental illness. Spiritual direction and personal therapy are essential. Authentic religion sets us free and renders us vulnerable to the divine energies. Unauthentic religious life cuts us off from the vital energy within our bodies and hearts and from intimate relationships with others, decreasing vulnerability and leading toward addiction.

Surviving in the Parish

Be involved in spiritual direction, mentoring, and personal therapy. Without a "pastor" figure, clergy cannot minister effectively to others. We learn to love and appreciate and guide and listen from having been loved and appreciated and guided and listened to. Spiritual direction, the confession, mentoring, and personal therapy are excellent means of support and facilitating spiritual growth.

Spend time with friends. Clergy must have ongoing opportunities for intimacy with peers where they can remove themselves from their role and speak freely and be received with understanding. For ministers who tend to be chronically isolated, the group experience fosters intimacy that helps make ministers less dependent on parishioners to meet personal needs. Ministers who cannot allow themselves to depend on others in legitimate ways for personal needs cannot expect to be free of the temptation to unconsciously (or deliberately) use members of the congregation to fill that role in inappropriate ways.

Eat a healthy diet. Three things can always be found at church gatherings: a Bible, coffee, and doughnuts. But remember, Jesus was a carpenter. He walked everywhere he went. There were no cars, planes, bicycles, televisions, or movies. Jesus' diet was natural and devoid of monodiglycerides and saturated fats. He was probably in good physical health and ate only fish, lean meat, grains, fruits, and vegetables—the kind of diet recommended by modern health practitioners. The church tradition of fasting is excellent not only as a spiritual discipline, but also for health reasons. At the very least, ministers should encourage healthy alternatives to the dull and deadly church social staples of coffee, doughnuts, and synthetic juices. Diet and exercise are vital to maintaining good mental and emotional health, especially when confronting a multitude of human problems on a daily basis.

Develop a hobby. Much of parish work is intangible. Doing something creative such as woodworking, pottery, painting, or music can offer a sense of accomplishment and refreshment. Outdoor activities such as cycling, gardening, swimming, running, horseback riding, hiking, and camping are good ways to wind down and celebrate the goodness of God evident through creation.

Reduce dependency on TV. Television is a mood-altering, trance-inducing drug that numbs the heart and opens the mind to a variety of cultural values of consumerism that are in direct conflict with the gospel. When possible, productive activities are to be preferred. Among these are: playing a musical instrument, painting, sculpting, woodworking, walking, journaling, playing sports, spending time with one's children, or having conversation with friends.

Participate in continuing education. Learning is a lifelong endeavor. Participation in seminars, workshops, and classes allows ministers the opportunity to rest from having to be the leader and provides time to enjoy the fellowship and exchange of ideas.

Take short retreats. A day or weekend or week spent at a monastery or retreat center allows time for silence and prayer and for the heart to rest between beats. Farmers let fields lie fallow to increase fertility. God recognized this need in all creation. Sabbath-keeping is a divine commandment. It is more than just "not working." It has to do with intentionally being present.

Notes

[1] E. H. Peterson, *Working the Angles: The Shape of Pastoral Integrity* (Grand Rapids: Eerdmans, 1987) 1-3.

[2] "Navel gazing" is condescendingly applied to psychophysiological techniques associated with various forms of meditation and yoga imported from other religions and resurfacing in the guise of so-called "New Age" practices. The term was actually coined by the Calabrian philosopher Barlaam, who attacked the age-old practice of silent continual inner prayer, which is the

heart of Eastern Orthodox Christian spiritual life and is widely practiced among the monastics, especially on Mount Athos. The theological basis of this method of prayer known as "hesychasm" was articulated definitively by St. Gregory Palamas in the fourteenth century in contradiction of Barlaam. Two church councils condemned Barlaam's viewpoints, and in so doing the Eastern Church avoided the problems affecting spiritual growth that developed in and through the spirit of the Renaissance and led eventually to the split between the physical and the "spiritual" and the reduction of prayer to a form of "discursive thinking" alone. For more on the historical and theological context of this controversy, see J. Meyendorff, *St. Gregory Palamas and Orthodox Spirituality* (New York: St. Vladimir's Seminary Press, 1974).

[3]S. Rabey, "Ministering to Ministers," *Colorado Springs Gazette Telegraph* (El Paso County) 13 February 1993, E1-2.

[4]Ibid.

[5]"Mano A'Mano," *AAPC Newsletter*, 31/3 (Summer 1993): 14.

[6]L. Dossey, *Meaning and Medicine* (New York: Bantam Books, 1991) 109.

[7]B. Siegel, *Peace, Love, and Healing* (New York: Harper & Row, Inc., 1989) 36.

[8]A. D. Goldberg, "The Sabbath: Implications for Mental Health," *Counseling and Values* 31/2 (1987): 147-54.

[9]D. Ornish, *Dr. Dean Ornish's Program for Reversing Heart Disease* (New York: Random House, 1990) 89.

[10]Ibid., 90.

[11]Ibid., 91.

[12]J. S. Muse and E. Chase, "Healing the Wounded Healers: 'Soul' Food for Clergy," in *Journal of Psychology and Christianity*, 12/2 (1993): 146.

[13]Cf. M. L. Morris and P. W. Blanton, "The Influence of Work-Related Stressors on Clergy Husbands and Their Wives," *Family Relations* 43 (April 1994): 189-95.

[14]Rabey, E1.

[15]R. E. Buxbaum, "When Pastors Divorce: A New Approach to Congregational Healing," *Journal of Pastoral Care* 49/2 (1995): 178.

[16]M. W. Frame and C. L. Shehan "Work and Well-Being in the Two-Person Career," *Family Relations* 43 (April 1994): 196-205.

[17]G. May, *Addiction and Grace* (San Francisco: Harper & Row, 1998).

[18]Cf. A. Bloom, *Beginning To Pray* (New York: Paulist Press, 1970).

[19]M. Woodman, "Worshiping Illusions: An Interview with Marion Woodman," *Parabola Magazine* 12/2 (1987): 56-57.

Suggested Readings

Kraybill, Donald B. *The Upside-Down Kingdom.* Scottdale PA: Herald Press, 1979. A rich re-creation of first-century Jerusalem that helps modern Americans understand the sociopolitical and economic milieu in which Jesus Christ lived. Emphasizes that twentieth-century Christianity has identified itself with pursuit of the American dream in ways that re-create many of the same dilemmas Jesus faced.

May, Gerald. *Addiction and Grace.* San Francisco: Harper & Row, 1988. A clear summary of the role of addiction that pervades every human life in every area. An important book for clergy who seek their own freedom and who help guide others along the same path.

Ornish, Dean. *Dr. Dean Ornish's Program for Reversing Heart Disease.* New York: Random House, 1990. An excellent summary of existing research on the relationship between love, intimacy, relaxation, and heart disease. Offers scientific evidence, methods for self-care, and dietary regimens that are healthy alternatives to a poor diet of emotional isolation, workaholism, and fast foods.

Oswald, Roy. *Clergy Self-Care.* New York: Alban Institute, 1991. An accurate picture of the common factors that weaken the parish ministry and practical helps for dealing with the problem.

Resources

Clergy Consultation Service
Blanton-Peale/Institutes of Religion and Health
212-725-7850

National Association of Religious Professionals (NARP) A special program of Ministers Life. Membership includes discounted subscriptions, telephone services, pharmacy service, vision plan, car care, travel, relocation services, and more (800-924-6277)

Turner Clergy Center
The Pastoral Institute
2022 15th Ave.
Columbus GA 31901
800-649-6446

Emmaus Journeys: The Medicine of Prayerful Encounters

Stephen Muse, Ph.D.

"He leads me beside still waters."

Who can be a minister to others without having a pastor for oneself? "I am the vine, you are the branches. . . . Apart from me you can do nothing." This chapter examines the place of confession, spiritual direction, mentoring, and personal therapy as "prayerful encounters" that are the seedbed for deepening compassion and discernment of clergy who would themselves offer the ministry of prayerful encounters to the Lord's flock.

Belovedness is the wellspring of pastoral energy and competence. The critical factor is not that we love God, but that God first loved us. Good pastoral care presumes a relationship with God that has healing, transforming, and sustaining power. No one can love others who has not first been loved. As our Lord pointed out to Simon the Pharisee, it is those who have been forgiven much who love much in return. As a matter of self-preservation and parish renewal, clergy must come to terms with the question: Who can minister to others without having a pastor for oneself?

Some ministers try to heal themselves by always being the helper. They allow others to come to them for guidance and a listening ear, but they do not permit the same for themselves. These pastors frequently use the helping relationship to bolster self-esteem and a flagging sense of self-worth. When it feels like a personal failure to have someone "help" you, it's time for serious reflection.

Ashamed of Being Human

I recall a minister who came to me for consultation. He was a strong, handsome man with a ready smile and a boyish charismatic charm—the kind of person to whom people respond favorably. After the door to my office closed on our first meeting, still smiling, he said, "I felt a little funny sitting in the waiting room. I was hoping none of my parishioners saw me here." "Why is that?" I asked, my clinical antennas coming up. He laughed and began to minimize his concern, reacting instantly to the fact that I noticed his remark as having some significance beyond what he perhaps had initially intended.

This man's anxiety over being "seen" by one of his parishioners had to do with the fact that they would be seeing him as someone human, who like themselves "needs help." In some sense, perhaps, it was a way of testing the waters to see if I would "look down" on him for seeking help. Because he was embarrassed and needed to hide his vulnerability from the sight of others, he would inevitably be counseling from a one-up position. This would leave those with whom he worked in a one-down position, perhaps without either of them realizing the subtle disempowering that could result. In fact, at that moment it was difficult for him to be with me. He could feel the unequal ground on which he was standing as he experienced our relationship through his own lenses.

Psychologically speaking, one of the consequences of "falling from grace" is that we seek our personal identities, not by acknowledging them as God-given moment by moment, but by comparing and positioning ourselves as different than and superior to others. For Adam and Eve in the Genesis account, the forbidden fruit of desiring to be "like God" replaced thanksgiving for being loved by God just as they were. Cain compared himself to Abel, and murder arose first in his heart and then in his deeds when he killed his brother out of envy. We must keep in mind that the evil of such envy, and every other passion, is at the root a distortion of love and the desire for restoration of intimacy with God, self, and others. The more we seek to separate it from grace, the deeper our imprisonment in the passions that further separate us.

Jesus, in contrast, though he was one with God, did not count this as something to be appropriated for himself as a human person. He was quick to question: "Why do you ask me about what is good? There is only one who is good" (Matt 19:17). Consequently, he was able to be fully human without pretense. He could weep, express anger, feel abandoned by God, and enjoy friendship. He could get on his knees and serve those who knew him as Master. He could call his disciples "friends," rather than behave like those in power who liked to lord it over others, separating themselves from those sinners who were considered beneath them. "It will not be so among you; but whoever wishes to be great among you must be your servant" (Matt 20:26-27). Christ's sense of self and approach to power meant that he could honestly say, "Come to me, all you that are weary and are carrying heavy burdens, and I will give you rest. . . . for I am gentle and humble in heart . . . For my yoke is easy, and my burden is light" (Matt 11:28). Such humility does not come from being unwilling to share oneself with others in similar ways. It is not built on self-definition, but on self-abandonment. God-esteem is more central than self-esteem. One becomes truly a self by abandoning the quest for self-definition in favor of a life that is obedient to grace. This type of obedience when invited by God's humility and goodness is completely different than obedience to one who coerces, forces, fascinates, or seduces the soul.

Perfection, as God intends for us, does not come from being what we are not, but from being authentically and totally what we are. Insomuch as God made us in the divine image, being ourselves and being obedient to God go hand in hand. If we try to "show off," we alienate ourselves from our true selves. "The glory of God," said St. Irenaus in the early second century, "is a human being fully alive." When asked, "What is the purpose of spiritual discipline?" St. Anthony in the early fourth century responded in a similar vein, "to become yourself." Freedom from relationship-destroying shame comes not from constant expectations of perfection from ourselves, but rather in allowing ourselves to be perfectly guileless with others.

The state of belovedness to God casts out all fear, for fear has to do with not being good enough. Fear has to do with reprisals expected for being less than that that for which God creates us. The beginning of this disease is accurately depicted in Genesis as shame at being ourselves, which is not good enough when we compare ourselves to God. When we are not willing to be ourselves, we are inevitably assuming the prerogative of God to re-create ourselves as some other. We are no longer in the arena of love and intimacy; we are more concerned with appearances. Control, fear, and a counterfeit charisma result.

Personal Charisma and the Holy Spirit

Salespeople fascinate me. They have an obvious agenda: to do their will. They want to sell me something. When there is a Hollywood sheen to them and the product is religion, I find it doubly fascinating. I was teasing a friend about this one day. He has a flair for the dramatic and is at ease entertaining a crowd. He said, "When my wife and I were in Las Vegas and Robert Goulet came on stage, his charisma filled up the whole place. My wife and I both recognized immediately why he's a star."

Interestingly, by contrast, when Malcolm Muggeridge interviewed Mother Teresa in the late 1960s, he remarked, "She has no charisma." He was then surprised by the fact that viewers of the program called in saying "That woman spoke to my heart in a way no other person ever has!" The charisma of the personality dominates Hollywood, television, and sadly, many of our churches, always playing to the audience for endorsement and exhortation. On the other hand, personal essence illuminated by the Holy Spirit is very different. The neon glitz and charm of personality are secondary and unremarkable when compared to the spiritual qualities of humility, goodness, and charity—which are magnets to the essence of others with ears tuned to the Shepherd's voice. "The sheep hear my voice. Other voices there will not follow." Ministers who lead with their personality may be creating in the sheep a flair for the dramatic, but are they reaching the heart as did Mother Theresa?

Offering the Medicine of Grace

The whole world is infected with the disease of "not-good-enoughness." In response, people frantically become involved in various kinds of entertainments and must-becomedness programs that polish and promote the cult of personality. In the midst of this, ministers are emissaries of the Christ who brings the message of grace and the curative medicine that pours from the cup of salvation and heals human disease and nourishes the human essence. In this ministry, clergy are invited to be human with and for others, not to be superhuman. To seek to be superhuman is to continue the old lie of the serpent in Genesis and to further damage persons who fail in comparison to their minister who appears to have it all together. The message to others is that by comparison "you are not yet good enough, but you can get better, and I have the means to help you." Inferiority is a kind of soul-infection, resulting in the diseases of must-becomedness and hypocrisy, which are barriers to love and intimacy.

For many in the helping professions, the motivation for compassion and empathy is fed in part by personal experiences of woundedness. Those who most deeply understand the suffering of others have themselves been deeply wounded and worked their way through their hurt by relying on the grace of God. Problems arise when the position of helper or minister is used to heal one's own wounds by segregating oneself from those who need ministry themselves.

Most people desire to have contact with the interior life of other humans, to move beyond the ordinary social boundaries. When ministers do not find this for themselves, the pastoral care they offer is easily contaminated, and their well-being and that of the parishioners is endangered. Ministers become vulnerable to over-identifying with the professional role of helper-of-others and to filling the emptiness inside with the one-way intimacy of the consulting room and Sunday morning worship. Over time, they become increasingly needy and eventually become dependent on those whose lives supply the emotional intensity that is missing from their own, while on the surface appearing more and more "together" by way of compensation.

The antidote to this disease is to remain needy with God by way of continual repentance. "Lord Jesus Christ, have mercy on me a sinner" has been the root of all prayers to God for two millenia. Even a quick perusal of the New Testament reveals a clear fact: People who do not feel sick do not look for a physician. It is the deaf, the blind, the lame, and the paralyzed who find new life in their encounters with Christ. Suffering leads people to God. Those who see do not seek to be given new eyes. Those who already feel they can accomplish everything do not seek healing for paralysis. In the midst of the crowd's disdain, it is the blind beggar Bartimaeus who cries out boldly, "Son of David, have mercy on me!" As a result, he is noticed and healed by Jesus. It is the woman who has been hemorrhaging for twelve years whose need and faith combine to draw power from the Lord merely by touching the hem of his garment.

Neediness is not a comfortable thought for Americans in the twenty-first century. Seeking to avoid the pitfalls of arrogance on the one hand and self-destroying despondency on the other, we focus on "self-esteem" and miss the ingredients of "God-esteem" and repentance that go together to heal both the soul and the community. Father Paisios, a respected elder from Mount Athos in Greece, has good advice regarding the right human attitude for prayer.

> A person should not place his intellect in the icon of Christ nor in the letters. He should place his intellect in his own sinfulness. Always with discretion, naturally, because many times the devil can do harm there also, telling him: "You are sinful, very sinful." Care is needed, for one to tell the devil: "What does it interest you? When I want, I will say that I am sinful, not when you want. One should always place one's intellect in his own sinfulness with hope in God. One becomes concentrated afterward: he feels the prayer as a need and says "Lord, Jesus Christ, have mercy on me."[1]

There is an emphasis on sinfulness that comes from the heart but that is released by the mercy, grace, and goodness of God who visits us in the humble love of His Son. This experience deepens our yearning for God. The human soul can bear this pain, and it is medicine that purifies and cures. Sinfulness can also come from outside the heart, whether by way of irrational childhood attributions of blame and self-hatred or from other persons in our lives who are ready to throw the stones of accusation. Sin opens the door to despondency, which eats away at hope and faith in God. We must turn away from such voices. Only God can convict sin in the human heart because only God is pure. Only God loves us with a love that experiences the weight of the sin within us and protects and heals us from the terrible pain involved in seeing ourselves in the bright, pure light of Christ.

Ours is a lifelong "continual repentance" until the last breath. When we continue in this truth, we become, like the Velveteen rabbit, more and more human. We may not look the way the world expects us to look, but we will be free. We will be alive the way God intends. This humanness, evidenced in the fruits of the spirit—peace, joy, long-suffering, kindness, faith, hope, reverence, love, and so on—is the best evangelism. God-illumined human nature is the vehicle that the Living God chose to use to become fully available to creation and to make a way for our return to communion with God. "A broken and contrite heart, O God, you will not despise" (Ps 51:17b). Or as the apostle Paul noted, we each have "treasure in clay jars." Our bodies are designed to be the temples of the Holy Spirit. Anything less fails to be authentically human.

The Power of Humanness

In contrast to the outward appearance of "having it all together" are the ministers whose humanity and vulnerability become vehicles for God's power to be manifest. I will always remember the priest who taught one of the first pastoral counseling courses I took in my graduate work in psychology. At the time I had been in parish work about three or four years. I expected a great deal of myself. I had not yet had personal therapy, and those who I assumed had it all together intimidated me. The more I learned, the wider became the gulf between what I imagined them to be and how I regarded myself. So my anxiety and nervousness in their presence became even greater, along with my unconscious need to measure up in order to get their blessing.

At any rate, one day as this priest was teaching, he began to weep. I don't remember what he was saying, but I do remember the tears—a spiritual man, a psychologist, and chair of the pastoral counseling department, a man in a position of authority, weeping like that in front of everyone. Prior to that time, I had been withholding expression of both my pain and my joy. Now here was someone I admired who was respected and who was suffering the humiliation of weeping in front of the class. I sought him out at the first opportunity to tell him how much his openness meant to me. It began an important mentoring relationship for me that gave me permission to allow my own vulnerability to become an avenue of healing for myself and others.

God works best through us not when we are superhuman, but when we are fully human. We must seek out relationships for ourselves that help us to live from our human essence if we are to be of help in facilitating this goal in others. This is the ministry of prayerful encounters, and it begins with receiving this for ourselves. Along with friendship, the Emmaus journeys of confession, spiritual direction, mentoring, and pastoral counseling are valuable means to do this.

The Sacrament of Confession

Cleopas and his friend walked with burning hearts on the road to Emmaus as they discussed the events of the past week concerning the crucified Lord. They talked with the stranger about Scripture and of what they most loved and grieved over. In the midst of this encounter they invited the stranger to have supper with them, where they found him breaking bread for them. Suddenly they recognized in him the Lord they loved.

God hears our confessions "where two or three are gathered in my name." Every time priests or ministers break bread with their congregations, those whose hearts burn with love will recognize an image of the Lord in their midst. This is the essential context of confession that for the more than one billion members of the Anglican, Eastern Orthodox, and Roman Catholic churches is considered an extension of the Eucharist . . . a sacrament uniting heaven and earth . . . an Emmaus journey.

In the ancient church there is a long tradition of spiritual direction that occurs in the context of the prayerful encounter of confession.[2] It is one thing to confess sins in the silence of the mind alone where sinful thoughts like "venomous reptiles" may still be kept in secret, often continuing to poison the heart; it is quite another to confess audibly to God in the presence of another human being. When I confess to God in the presence of another person my failures to live the commandments of Christ, to love others and live out a total response to the gift of his body and blood, I am present in such a way that my body responds to the truth of my lips and powerful feelings emerge. An experienced confessor and abbot of one of the monasteries on Mount Athos extols the power of confession that releases curative forces of grace that open a person to deeper self-awareness and spiritual growth:

> A spiritual operation is undoubtedly painful while being carried out but without this psychical pain the wicked pleasure of sin cannot be exterminated nor can our minds be rid of the invisible fetters of guilt. The shame felt by the (person) confessing at that moment is only temporary, while at the same time it is doubly rewarding. From the moment he confesses openly and without excuses, the (person) who has a sense of his sinfulness is redeemed both by this court of conscience, of which nothing in the world is stricter, and by the Court of the Judgement to come. Besides, so much grace takes up the emptied space after this spiritual rendering up that it is sufficient to reward not only the one confessed, but there is also enough of it to urge him to look deeper inside to force those venomous reptiles to come out and stop poisoning his heart.[3]

A Contemporary Example

Alexander Ogarodnikov, a Russian prisoner of conscience during the Soviet communist years, who returned to Christianity after years of disillusionment in Marxism, tells of his encounter with an old Russian monk during confession that changed his life. The old man listened intently to his story with tears of understanding and shared sorrow inspired by God in a heart made humble by his own tireless repentance and confessions. Ogarodnikov was moved to the depths by the grace of God in the presence of this old man's love and humility and began to be aware of parts of his life he had long forgotten. The door to a new life opened when he made his first confession; and he found it was also, as St. John Chrysostom observed, the doorway to the kingdom of heaven, which had been alluding him in the glitz and glamour of the churches he had visited. Of this experience he wrote:

> I went to the Pskov Cave Monastery to confess before an elder who was 92 years old. He confessed me for seven hours! As he was listening to my confession, tears continued to flow and flow for seven hours out of his eyes. I don't recall it exactly now, but apparently I remembered my whole life—my *whole* life. It seems to me I even remembered things I was unconscious of having done. I felt as if a huge weight had been lifted off my chest. The rest of the night until

the early morning liturgy I couldn't sleep. I walked around the monastery grounds and even went outside the walls of the monastery. I was filled with so much joy I wanted to yell to the stars. In the morning I partook of Holy Communion.[4]

This is the place of the prayerful encounter where the medicine of grace is offered to weary pilgrims as an antidote to sin and the disease of must-becomedness. The slate is cleared, and I am reoriented to the sacredness of life just as it is in the moment here and now—the only moment for which I can be responsible. Those who would participate in hearing confessions must themselves receive the same gift frequently.

Spiritual Direction

A minister once called me seeking "spiritual direction" as distinct from psychotherapy. He was clear about the difference between the two and what he was wanting from me. Unsure whether he was seeking a listening ear and a confirming word of God's presence as distinct from a contract for therapeutic change, I suggested we meet in my office during my lunchtime. That way it left me free not to charge a fee until we had determined the nature of his request.

Looking forward to being with someone with a clear mandate to attend to the presence of God in contrast to diagnosing pathology and seeking change, I noticed that on the morning of our intended meeting my prayers were more focused and alive than usual, and my intention to be still inside was more available to me. When the minister arrived, I sat on the sofa where my clients usually sit in order to avoid the customary physical sensations and impressions linked to my habitual place of seeing clients as a "professional counselor." I imagine Jesus as not being "professional" so much as intimately "personal," albeit dispassionatley so.

I relaxed a little more and changed my body posture in an effort to be present with this person before God and to attend to the movement of the Holy Spirit in his life and with us in the moment. My diagnostic and therapeutic arsenal were present, but more on the back burner as I tried to be attentive to us in God's presence.

At times I noticed my thumb and the forefinger of my right hand moving in circles in the rhythm of my mind sifting through diagnostic considerations, and I had to remind myself I was seeking to listen in a different way. We had what seemed like a very intimate and valuable meeting, and the man appeared to be deeply thoughtful about what had transpired. His sincere search for God and his willingness to be open with me called forth an attending presence and listening heart from me that were different in quality from what is often there for my clients (who are often in search of things such as freedom from depression, a better relationship, or to overcome panic attacks). We both loved Christ. This presence of mind did not totally dissipate, but it lingered with me for the rest of the day. I found myself praying silently for my other clients as I sat with them, even after I had moved back to my ordinary seat and was working with them in my accustomed way. I found I was present with them more than I am usually able to achieve. A prayerful attention similar to oxygen that brings everything else into refreshing new life was present.

In a small measure this was an echo of what I have experienced following my own personal confessions. I weep with gratitude and feel joyful sorrow and feel the faith-renewed recognition of my own frailty. A desire for prayer fanned into a gentle flame. I have noticed on several occasions that on the day following confession, my pastoral counseling seemss to have more empathy and compassion. Subjectively I feel I have more love and appreciation for the personhood of my clients than I did before and that they make better progress. Perhaps the context of grace is more palpable. "You received without payment; give without payment" (Matt 10:8b). What is more healing than to be noticed as we are and embraced by grace conveyed through a personal human relationship gratefully in the presence of God?

To the degree that the minister's Christian faith is alive, nourished by the sacraments or ordinances, connected to a worshiping community and aware of God's abiding presence—revivified in an ongoing relationship of confession, spiritual direction, and prayerful attention—therapeutic relationships offered by that minister are subtly changed. I believe this spirit along with the context of mutual vulnerability before God, empowered by shared Christian faith, is what makes the ministry of pastoral relationships uniquely healing.

Regardless of a professional's theoretical orientation, empathy and compassion have been shown repeatedly to be the most important healing ingredients in therapy.[5] Furthermore, empathy has been shown to be significantly related to the quality of religious maturity of the therapist, which appears to be in part a function of the therapist having experienced a continuing relationship of love and empathy with God over time through difficult circumstances.[6]

I know personally how much I benefit from having confession and spiritual direction from one who has devoted his life to prayer and worship and himself received a similar guidance from an experienced mentor. The role of spiritual direction for clergy is a critical issue because we live in a world increasingly dominated by corporate interests of consumption and materialism, and the churches must live out an alternative to this. Otherwise, the church becomes a mere extension of the world and the clergy representatives of Madison Avenue and secular psychological schools with their ethos, values, and assumptions about the purpose of human life.

In contrast, Metropolitan Heirotheos Vlachos,[7] following St. Basil's lead, argues that the Christian church is essentially a hospital, the priests are psychotherapists, and the Sacraments (along with worship, doctrine, and asceticism) are medicines. Properly administered and received, the medicine of Christian faith and relationship is a powerful intervention. If clergy are to administer it properly, they must also receive it for themselves. Spiritual direction for ministers is a means of quality assurance for those they serve.

Personal Therapy

In many ways ministers have uncritically embraced the values and methods of psychotherapy. However, psychotherapy is a tool to use, not a religion to embrace uncritically.[8] While there is overlap between the two, there are also important distinctions of context and methodology between psychotherapy and spiritual direction that serve distinct, though complimentary, aims.

One author in a recent article appearing in the *American Psychologist* observed that "psychology is, in American society, filling the void created by the waning influence of religion in answering questions of ultimacy and providing moral guidance."[9] Protestant theology itself has in many ways been changed by psychology and the value systems and methodologies implicit in them from what it attempted to be in the beginning. In a survey of the American religious scene, sociologist Robert Bellah observed:

> The quasi-therapeutic blandness that has afflicted much of mainline Protestant religion at the parish level for over a century cannot effectively withstand the competition of the more vigorous forms of radical religious individualism, with their claims of dramatic self-realization, or the resurgent religious conservatism that spells out clear, if simple, answers in an increasingly bewildering world.[10]

In the past half-century, American religious life has become increasingly a culture of the therapeutic, reinterpreting the meaning and value of love, marriage, family, personal growth, and commitment in highly individualistic ways that often depart significantly from traditional Christian ethos and values.

Bridging Psychology and Spiritual Direction

Spiritual direction involves a clear focus on the belovedness of persons in the sight of God. It is an open-ended attentiveness to the presence and workings of the Holy Spirit in human life without any attempt to change or influence that life in any way. Spiritual direction is a witness to God's grace active in a particular human life. It is an antidote to "must-becomedness," a reorienting to "just-beingness" in the context of a soul's belovedness to God.

Secular psychotherapy's emphasis on pathological diagnosis and cure often shifts the ground away from being to becoming and subtly reinfects persons with the disease of not-good-enoughness. Good pastoral counseling is a bridge between the world of empirical science and the world of religious conviction and values. Pastoral counseling can help clergy clear away obstacles to spiritual growth, returning them to the path of spiritual formation.

During my early training in counseling, while I was pastor of a church, a man called and asked me to see him as both pastor and psychotherapist. It was important for him that I have on both hats, so to speak, to view him and his experience with clinical acumen through the lens of our shared Christian faith. He wanted both a scientist and a priest to attend to him and his situation. The difference between these two tasks as well as the important overlap between them became very clear to me in our subsequent interaction.

He was a very bright man who was having marital problems a few years after the "happiest day of my life" when he had married the first woman he had ever loved who had not been a prostitute. I was aware that he had much guilt about his previous relationships with women and that he tended to suppress his feelings chronically. His wife had lost interest in him and found a younger man at a local bar. Marriage counseling had been unsuccessful.

Over the years I had made some pastoral calls on him and his wife and had a sense of the context and the depth of his suffering. Sitting with him, I saw that his pain was tremendous and called for more than a simple empathic response. I asked him to read Psalm 51 aloud. As he slowly read, he had a massive conversion of heart with outpouring of feelings and, I believe, avoided a major depression or nervous break-down. He told me later he got lost on the way home, drunk with feeling, and his whole life changed after that. He attended church regu-larly and after moving out of state kept in contact with me for several years. I am so thankful that his "conversion" came in relationship with God's word and with me as both pastor and therapist. I am grateful for his Christian faith and for the grace of the moment when the fruit is ripe, which cannot be orchestrated except by God.

Mentoring

When I received a call to my first parish as solo pastor, I learned of a group of other pastors who met weekly to study the Bible together in preparation for preaching each Sunday. I was full of energy and alive with idealistic fervor, so attending the group at first was not a high priority for me. An older pastor from an adjoining town invited me to ride with him thirty miles to attend the group meeting on a weekly basis. We brought a sack lunch and talked during the ride. I did so at first with a mild interest. Ten years later I attended each week with alacrity, affection, gratitude, and interest in the small ecumenical group of clergy who came from a fifty-mile area to study the lectionary for the week, sharpen one another's minds, bear one another's burdens, and pray for the welfare of the church in all places.

When it avoids being a "bitch-and-brag" session, clergy gatherings can be some of the most powerful experiences of faith available to ministers—an Emmaus gathering of disciples who truly believe, who truly struggle to live the faith and serve the people of God. Where intimacy and collegiality prevail, sustenance and inspiration and continuing pastoral and personal growth are givens.

This particular group began with a group of pastors who hired a psychiatrist to facilitate a group that discussed pastoral issues and case studies from their respective parishes. As they learned to balance pastoral care and clinical awareness, they grew to love and trust each other. When the psychiatrist left the area, the pastors decided to continue meeting and to change their focus to the task of preaching. The group had been going for some twenty years when I left, and I suspect it continues today.

The forty-minute drive to and from the group offered me a mentoring relationship with a mature man who had thirty years of pastoral experience. It wasn't so much "how-tos" and "what-nots" that were valuable, but rather the confidence and trust this older man placed in me and the reciprocal relationship from which he himself benefited. The group members also provided mentoring on a more casual basis, with various members contributing from time to time according to each one's gift and the leading of the Spirit. The group provided a safe place to cry, to tell of family tragedy and professional problems, to make confession, and to share the joys of ministry that all would understand and appreciate.

It is nonsense to try to minister in a congregation without having colleagues with whom to meet on a regular basis for consultation, prayer, and fellowship. Support groups with a focus specifically on support sometimes lack the leadership and direction necessary to endure unless the depth of sharing is significant. Finding a group with a shared task of preparing for ministry together can often succeed in also offering support and intimacy. Those who work together and pray together tend to stay together.

Our lectionary group held silent retreats twice a year, facilitated by one or two of the members. We celebrated Eucharist together, laughed and wept and pondered. We exchanged pulpits, shared Lenten lecture series, and sometimes took trips together. The group linked together several geographical and denominational communities in ways that otherwise would not have occurred. When one member of the group left for a new parish, he or she received a going-away dinner that, as the group increased in size, began to involve regular social gatherings with spouses. The ministry can be a lonely place, and ministers, like the military or law enforcement, can become a sort of fraternity that appreciates and understands the uniqueness of one another's callings, creating a vital connection with one another.

Contemplative Groups

Group silence has also been an important means of support for me, though harder to come by. In Washington, D.C., the Shalem Institute for Spiritual Formation attracts a number of persons interested in spiritual formation, contemplative prayer, workshops, and ongoing groups. Being part of a small group that regularly keeps silent vigil together and shares personal struggles and experiences along the way is also a vital support. Parish ministry is demanding, and time for quiet prayer is easily co-opted for more task-oriented action. Contemplative prayer groups help keep the flame of prayer alive on a weekly basis. Without it, daily mindfulness that supports all other pastoral work is sometimes lost, and with that loss begins the loss of all the rest.

Remaining authentic, alive and growing in parish ministry means maintaining a vital human life. Contemplative groups provide an ongoing act of love that is fully present to life in the context of God's active grace. In contrast to the burgeoning self-help psychology mentality, the ministry of prayerful encounters helps ministers remain attentive to how Christ is already functioning in their lives by sharing their humanity with others. Eugene Peterson speaks of finding grace in the "unlikely places" of our ordinary lives when he describes the pastor's job as not to solve people's problems or to make them happy, but to help them see the grace operating in their lives.

> It's hard to do, because our whole culture is going the other direction, saying that if you're smart enough and get the right kind of help, you can solve all your problems. The truth is, there aren't very many happy people in the Bible. But there are people who are experiencing joy, peace, and the meaning of Christ's suffering in their lives.[11]

The work of spirituality is to recognize the particular circumstances of our lives and to recognize grace and say, "Do you suppose God wants to be with me in a way that does not involve changing my spouse or getting rid of my spouse or my kids, but in changing me and doing something in my life that maybe I could never experience without this pain and suffering?" Such attentiveness is best given to others when clergy are intentional about receiving it for themselves.

Notes

[1]Fr. Paisios, "A Conversation with the Elder: Father Paisios of Mount Athos," *Divine Ascent: A Journal of Orthodox Faith* 3/4 (1998): 96.

[2]Cf. J. Allen, *Inner Way: Toward a Rebirth of Eastern Christian Spiritual Direction* (Grand Rapids: Eerdmans, 1994).

[3]Fr. Ephraim, *A Call From the Holy Mountain* (Blanco TX: New Sarov Press, 1991) 27.

[4]A. Ogarodnikov, "Interview with a Russian Prisoner of Conscience," in *Again* 13/1: 5.

[5]H. Strupp, "The Therapist's Theoretical Orientation: An Overrated Variable," *Psychotherapy:Theory, Research, and Practice* 15 (1978): 315.

[6]J. S. Muse, B. K. Estadt, J. M. Greer, and S. Cheston, "Are Religiously Integrated Therapists More Empathic?" *Journal of Pastoral Care* 48/1 (1994): 14-23.

[7]Cf. H. Vlachos, *Orthodox Psychotherapy of the Soul* (Greece: Birth of the Theotokos* Monastery, 1994).

[8]Cf. S. Muse, "Orthodox Psychotherapy: A Marriage Made in Heaven or a House Divided?" and "Response to Dr. Ana Maria Rizzuto's 'In Spirit and in Truth'" *Personhood: Deepening the Connections Between Body, Mind, and Soul,* J. Chirban, ed. (Greenwich CT: Bergin & Garvey Publishers, 1995) 61-81.

[9]S. L. Jones, "A Constructive Relationship for Religion with the Science and Profession of Psychology," *American Psychologist* 49/3 (1994): 192.

[10]R. Bellah, et. al, *Habits of the Heart* (Berkeley: University of California Press, 1985) 238.

[11]E. Peterson, personal communication.

Suggested Readings

Allen, J. *Inner Way: Toward a Rebirth of Eastern Christian Spiritual Direction.* Grand Rapids: Eerdmans, 1994. Evidences 2,000-year history of spiritual direction as practiced within the Eastern Orthodox Church. Excellent resoure for those seeking to serve as a spiritual guide to others.

Anonymous. *The Way of a Pilgrim.* R. M. French, trans. New York: Ballantine, 1974. A rare and beautiful book written by an anonymous nineteenth-century Russian Orthodox pilgrim who discovers the secret of continual prayer. The humble author's simplicity and sincerity, along with his remarkable story, are a powerful evangel of the grace of God whose love he shares with the reader.

Bloom, Anthony. *Beginning To Pray.* New York: Paulist Press, 1970. A modern classic by the Russian Orthodox physician-priest and now Archbishop of Western Europe. The author's concrete, practical style and his own authentic spiritual discernment render his observations fresh and helpful, especially for persons seeking to find a Christian path in the marketplace.

Bondi, R. C. *To Pray and To Love: Conversations on Prayer with the Early Church.* Minneapolis: Augsburg/Fortress Press, 1991. A refreshing journey through the desert fathers and mothers with commentary and reflection by a modern female pastor and theologian.

Edwards, T. *Spiritual Friend: Reclaiming the Gift of Spiritual Direction.* New Jersey: Paulist Press, 1980. Very practical book on spiritual direction. Written by an Episcopal priest who founded the highly successful Shalem Institute for Spiritual Formation. Includes an excellent bibliography of related resources.

Fisher, K. *Women at the Well: Feminist Perspective on Spiritual Direction.* New York: Paulist Press, 1988. A helpful book not only for women, but also for male ministers who offer spiritual counsel to women. Includes suggestions for prayer and reflection at the end of each chapter. Easily used in retreat settings.

Foster, R. J. *Celebration of Discipline: The Path to Spiritual Growth.* New York: Harper & Row, 1978. A helpful primer on the classical disciplines of Christian formation.

Groeschel, B. J. *Spiritual Passages: The Psychology of Spiritual Development.* New York: Crossroad, 1988. A view of human development beginning with birth and proceeding through the classical Western Christian path of "purgation, illumination, and union" with Christ in God.

Jenkins, J. M. *The Ancient Laugh of God: Divine Encounters in Unlikely Places.* Louisville KY: Westminster/John Knox Press, 1994. Essays on the life of earth and common human experience illuminated by the grace of God.

Jones, Alan *Soul Making: The Desert Way of Spirituality.* New York: Harper & Row, 1985. Drawing on the desert fathers, contains solid and thoughtful direction in spiritual life from an experienced pastor. Notes difference between psychological help and spiritual direction and how they work together.

Lawrence, B. *The Practice of the Presence of God*, trans. by E. M. Blaiklock. Nashville: Thomas Nelson Publishers, 1981. A very readable volume from a cook who found God's presence everywhere and prayed even while flipping pancakes.

May, Gerald. *Care of Mind/Care of Spirit: Psychiatric Dimensions of Spiritual Direction.* New York: Harper & Row, 1982. A balanced, informative guide to the psychological side of spiritual guidance. Written from a psychiatrist's viewpoint, demonstrates appreciation for the role of psychotherapy as a tool within the larger context of religious formation.

Peterson, E. H. *Working the Angles: The Shape of Pastoral Integrity.* Grand Rapids: Eerdmans, 1987. A clarion call to reorient one's pastoral ministry to the classical calling of prayer, Scripture, and spiritual direction. A challenge to the model of Christian ministry that is a sell-out to sociology, success, and the American dream. Includes several excellent chapters on spiritual direction.

Sabbaticals: Methods and Motives

James Johnson, D.Min.

"He restores my soul."

A veteran pastor reflects on the role of Sabbath as a support for a long and successful career. Reflecting on personal experience, he offers practical suggestions toward making an extended leave from the parish possible for ministers in churches who may not be used to the idea of sabbaticals.

Upon hearing that a prominent pastor in his city, at age 51, was leaving the ministry, an enterprising reporter asked, "Why?" The minister replied: "I have decided that I am going to retire from active, formal ministry. Before I die, before my life ends on this planet, I want to experience some life each week of which contains some portion of time that I can keep and protect and count on just for me to do whatever I and my family may want to do without needing to be available and responsive to the needs of 3,500 other people . . . With no other church anywhere to which I would want to go, my alternative at age 51, having been here for eight years is to stay here for the next 14 years until I reach the age of 65. If I do that, dear friends, I would die."[1]

Perhaps this pastor's answer stirs you as it did me possibly because on more than one occasion I have felt the same way. I am equipped to write this chapter on sabbatical leaves as a way to restore one's soul, not because I have ever taken one, but because I should have, but was afraid to. I surmise that there are a multitude of ministers who sincerely need a sabbatical, and my purpose in this chapter is to encourage and equip you to do so. After all, the idea of a sabbatical rest is built into our creation. As Genesis 2:1-2 says, "Thus the heavens and the earth were finished and all their multitude. And on the seventh day God finished the work that he had done, and he rested on the seventh day from all the work that he had done."

God's chosen people understood this rest initiated by God to apply not only to humans, but also to God's creatures and the land. The Old Testament Law points out the importance of giving the land a rest from cultivation every seven years.

Academia has long recognized the value of the sabbatical for professors and teachers. Most foreign mission boards of American churches insist that their overseas missionaries take a year of furlough after four to six years overseas. The tradition and manifest value of a sabbatical should commend it to the serious consideration of every fully engaged minister.

There are manifold ways a minister's soul may be restored. In this chapter we will examine one of these ways, the sabbatical. We are not talking about the typical one month's vacation that most ministers receive, but frequently end up not taking. We are talking about an extended leave of a minimum of three months to a year.

Why at least three months? Anything less will not be long enough for the sabbatical to accomplish its intended purpose of restoring the minister's soul. To be restored, ministers must truly let go of their pastoral responsibilities for a time and focus their attention elsewhere.

Most ministers have experienced the circumstance of being called home from a vacation to attend to a pastoral care need such as comforting a bereaved family and conducting a funeral service. It is indeed the exception that ministers may enjoy a vacation without some contact with their parish. However, if it is understood by all concerned that they are engaged in a sabbatical leave for which careful plans have been made and that will involve them in an ongoing project, it will not be necessary to be reintroduced into the pressures of the pastorate prematurely, thereby defeating the purpose of the sabbatical.

For example, Eugene H. Peterson, pastor of Christ Our King Presbyterian Church in Bel Air, Maryland, insists that "his aim in life is merely being a dependable pastor." In an interview for *Christianity Today*, Peterson revealed that his sabbatical in northwest Montana—where he spent leisurely hours in prayer, hiking, reading, skiing, and writing—refreshed him and geared him up for a return to his pastoral work where he has "dedicated himself to the unsung promotion of honesty, simplicity, and substance."[2]

Negotiating a Sabbatical

If you have determined that you need a sabbatical, how do you go about getting one? The ideal way, of course, is to see that provision for a sabbatical leave is established at the time you are called to serve a church. It can be a part of the compensation package, which typically includes salary, housing allowance, education allowance, and pension and medical insurance premium payments. One pastor asked the church calling him to include in his compensation package a provision that two weeks sabbatical leave would accrue to him for every year he served the church. At the end of six years he had accrued twelve weeks of sabbatical leave. During his seventh year of service this time was added to his regular one-month vacation, and he engaged in a four-month sabbatical.

What if you did not plan ahead and negotiate a provision for a sabbatical at the time of your beginning service in a new church? Admittedly, under these circumstances a sabbatical will be more difficult to arrange, but it can be done.

After five or six years the people in your congregation will know you for better or for worse. They will be prepared to respond knowledgeably to your request for a sabbatical. If your people love and appreciate you, they will be open to the possibility of a sabbatical for you, provided that a few practical questions can be answered satisfactorily. After five or six years, if they don't know you and love you, then you probably don't need a sabbatical because you won't have been working all that hard in serving them.

To secure a sabbatical, considerable advance preparation is necessary—probably as much as six months. When you first introduce the idea of a sabbatical to your official board or other decision-making body, be prepared to answer all kinds of practical and spiritual questions, but do not require a decision for at least three months. The notion of a sabbatical, with pay, will take time to sink into the minds of the decision makers in your congregation.

Educating the Parish

First and most important, you need to establish a reason for requesting a sabbatical. Rarely do church members understand the stress under which their minister lives. They will never know unless you tell them, not in a complaining mood, but in a loving mood, from the point of view of wanting to serve them better.

In the illustration at the beginning of this chapter, we have an example of a pastor who appeared to his people to be so competent, motivated, and fulfilled that it occurred to none of them that he was near the breaking point. When he announced to his congregation that he was leaving the ministry, a member of the committee that nominated him as pastor eight years earlier said, "I'm surprised, very surprised. He's been so totally involved with what's been going on at [the church]."[3] One cannot help but wonder if this pastor had asked for a sabbatical after five or six years, he might still be in the ministry effectively serving a church that desperately wanted his leadership.

Requesting a Sabbatical

Sometimes ministers refrain from telling their church members they need a sabbatical for fear that such a need will show weakness or lack of dedication. These ministers need to call to mind what Jesus told his disciples after they had been extremely busy obeying their Master's command to proclaim that all should repent: "Come away to a deserted place all by yourselves and rest a while" (Mark 6:31), or what he said in Matthew 11:28, "Come to me, all you that are weary and are carrying heavy burdens, and I will give you rest." Surely it is no sign of lack of dedication to heed our Master's call to rest.

Or perhaps ministers refrain from asking for a sabbatical for fear that things will not be done right in the parish while they are away for an extended period of time. This attitude, often called "a messiah complex," is far from what Jesus had in mind for the church. No one, except Christ, is indispensable. The apostle Paul said in 2 Corinthians 4:6-7,

It is the God . . . who has shone in our hearts to give light of the knowledge of the glory of God in the face of Jesus Christ. But we have this treasure in clay jars, so that it may be made clear that this extraordinary power belongs to God and does not come from us.

For ministers to assume that their leadership is indispensable is to take unto themselves the glory that belongs to God.

If you need and want a sabbatical, explain that often when everyone else is relaxing and in a holiday mood—such as at Thanksgiving or Christmas or Easter—you are working harder than ever. Explain your desire to be available to the people during their time of need, but that vacations are sometimes interrupted, cut short, or eliminated by pastoral emergencies. Explain how time to study and think is hard to find in the midst of administrative and pastoral responsibilities and that you want the congregation to benefit from thoughtful sermons, energetic pastoral care, and wise administrative decisions—benefits that are more likely to arise when you are at your best.

Financing a Sabbatical

In addition to explaining the reason why you need a sabbatical, you will need to address the issue of cost. If yours is a multiple staff church, you should have already consulted with your colleagues to see how your duties may be divided in your absence. If you are the only staff member, greater ingenuity may be required.

With regard to pastoral care duties, you may learn from physicians who are in a solo practice. They simply arrange with a colleague to cover for them on specified occasions. A minister of the same or even of another denomination may be enlisted to visit your church members in the hospital.

With regard to administrative duties, laypersons need to be enlisted and equipped to make necessary decisions or to insure inquiring people that decisions will be made promptly and fairly when you return. By delegating some of these ministerial administrative duties, two valuable benefits may result: (1) The church people will achieve a greater appreciation for the complexity of the administrative tasks with which you must contend daily. (2) The church's future response to any challenge or opportunity to serve may be more effective because it is coming from more than one person (the minister), whose vision or experience may be limited.

With regard to preaching duties, if all added expenses must be avoided, you may need to secure capable lay speakers to fill the pulpit, either from your own church or from a neighboring church, even of a different denomination. Other possibilities are to find a retired minister in the community, a hospital chaplain, a military chaplain, a furloughed missionary, or a denominational executive to fill the pulpit one or more times.

Another possibility is an overseas pulpit exchange. A minister from an English-speaking country such as Canada, Australia, New Zealand, Nigeria, Great Britain, Ireland, or Belize could be invited to live in your home and preach in your church. You would in turn live in that person's home and serve her or his congregation. Admittedly, this is not a complete sabbatical, but it would be a complete change of scenery and probably not require any administrative duties nor the writing of new sermons every week. In addition, the contact with another culture could also be very enlightening and invigorating.

I know of one pastor who read in a Christian periodical of a minister in Scotland who was looking for a pulpit exchange for the summer with an American pastor. He answered the notice, engaged in a lengthy correspondence with the Scottish minister, and worked out, through letters and telephone calls, the details of an extremely beneficial pulpit exchange. Not only did he and his family enjoy a glorious summer in Scotland, but he also returned home to discover that his American congregation had been entranced by its Scottish pastor who had introduced it to some new ways of looking at the gospel and how it should be proclaimed.

Adopting a Positive Attitude

After the cost of a sabbatical is addressed, you may have to deal with feelings of guilt and fear. You may ask yourself, "How can I deal with my guilt if I abandon my people for a few months?" An antidote to this feeling is to ask yourself, "How can I deal with my guilt if I abandon my people permanently because I simply burn out?" The sabbatical should be viewed not as an abandonment, but as an equipping time. If you can be convinced that you can serve your people better from the point of view of personal wholeness, physical vigor, renewed enthusiasm, and spiritual depth, your people will catch your mood and see that it is in the best interest of the church for you to engage in a sabbatical leave.

Here is an extremely positive way to view a sabbatical, positive for you as the minister and positive for the congregation you serve. It has been observed that ministers who are discouraged, weary, or disappointed in one parish often overcome these emotions simply by moving to another parish. This is a rather wasteful manner in which to reinvigorate the minister. Very likely the church from which the minister has departed will need to engage the services of an interim pastor for twelve to eighteen months, during which time no new projects should be undertaken. It will take a new pastor a year or so to become confident about his or her leadership style and direction. Under these circumstances it would be less costly in time wasted and money spent to give the minister a sabbatical. In a year or less, the same minister who knows her or his congregation can plunge directly back into the work with confidence, knowledgeability, and renewed vigor.

Some ministers who need a sabbatical will hesitate to ask for one because of the fear that there may be unfortunate repercussions. They may fear that their detractors will say, "Look, we have a pastor who is not up to the responsibilities of this parish. If this is the way s/he feels, perhaps we should look for another pastor."

If you are experiencing this type of fear, take into your confidence a few reliable church members whose judgment you can trust and ask them if there is a serious risk if you ask for a sabbatical. If there is a risk, then there is a problem other than the need for a sabbatical. Problems with the perceived antagonists should be solved before thinking about planning a sabbatical.

Using a Sabbatical

After you have sufficiently dealt with feelings of guilt and fear, you will have to decide how to use the sabbatical. There are many valid options, the choosing of which will depend upon you and your family's needs. For example, some seminaries have a continuing education program that will provide meals and housing for you and perhaps your family. If intellectual stimulation is what you need, this would be a good option for your sabbatical.

On the other hand, if you have a family, you may discover that you need some extended time together. If you have younger children or teenagers, the summer months would be the obvious choice of when to take your sabbatical. Staying at home would be the cheapest, but perhaps the least helpful way to be together. Inevitably, pastoral demands would arise, and your children would want to maintain their contacts with their friends, and it would soon be "business as usual."

The cheapest, and often the most fruitful, way to be together as a family would be some variation of family camping. For the price of a trailer hitch installed on the family car, the rental of a "popup" camper, and the purchase of a guidebook to America's family campgrounds, you could possibly spend the most exciting summer of your lives.

Sometimes parishioners who own vacation homes may rise to the occasion and invite you to enjoy their hospitality. Naturally, you would not be likely to be invited to stay three months at any one place, but a judicious scheduling of responses to several invitations might cover the entire sabbatical time for you. It would have to become known throughout the congregation that you are open to receiving such invitations. Consequently, advance announcements and planning are essential.

Another option would be to join the summer staff of an organization, such as the National Council of Churches, that sponsors a chaplaincy program in our national parks. Also, you may want to consult your travel agent concerning cruise lines that furnish chaplaincy services.

For a contemplative sabbatical, you could consider a stay at one of the many monasteries in America or abroad. It is not necessary for you to be a member of the same denomination that operates the monastery. The Episcopal, Greek Orthodox, Lutheran, and Roman Catholic churches all operate monasteries of varying degrees of strictness of conduct. Consult a clergy member of one of these denominations to secure a list of the monasteries operated by his/her communion.

The vestry of a particular Episcopal church approved an unusual sabbatical for its priest. Because he was serving an urban church in a community of about 200,000 people, he thought it would be beneficial to visit other urban churches with successful programs to see what ministries of these churches contributed to their growth in numbers and in spirituality. The vestry was very pleased with this idea for the minister's sabbatical and was also pleased to provide funding for it. At the end of the sabbatical the priest gave a detailed report of his findings and recommendations to the vestry, which then proceeded to implement those it considered to be most feasible. If you are contemplating a sabbatical, you might be well advised to undertake a study project that would benefit both yourself and your congregation. The process of exploring together what would be a suitable sabbatical project would undoubtedly garner wider support for the whole idea of a sabbatical and would bring greater long-term benefits for the congregation.

Eliminating Risks

Learning of a colleague who had recently taken a four-month sabbatical leave, this writer asked him how he managed it. Here is a paraphrase of his reply:

> In a previous parish, after about eight years, I was nearly burned out. My bishop came to my rescue, saying to the vestry, "You have a priest who has served you well. You would prefer to have him continue to serve you, rather than go through the difficult and costly process of looking for a new rector. I recommend that you give this man a sabbatical leave. Afterwards he will come back to you renewed in physical health and spiritual vigor." The vestry acted favorably on the bishop's recommendation, and I enjoyed the first sabbatical of my ministerial career. When I received a call to my present parish, I asked the vestry to include in my compensation provisions for a sabbatical. After five years' service here I had accrued enough time to take a sabbatical. However, a new associate rector had just come, and I delayed my sabbatical for a year while my associate found his way in the parish, gained the confidence of the people, and demonstrated that he could serve capably while I was away.

If, for any reason, you are hesitant about asking for a sabbatical in your current situation, wait for a call to the next congregation you will serve. As you discuss salary, housing arrangements, and reimbursement for professional expenses such as auto travel and insurance coverage, also discuss provision for a sabbatical. If such a provision is built into the terms of your call, then everyone will understand why you are taking a sabbatical when the appropriate time for it arrives.

Obviously, planning an affordable and fruitful sabbatical will require considerable ingenuity and much time. Only you can decide if it is worth the effort. The best way to make sure that it will not be counterproductive is to discuss the idea of a sabbatical with your family and the leaders of your church far in advance of the time for the sabbatical. If you receive general consent, then start your planning, reassured by the remembrance that even our Savior and his disciples felt the need for a sabbatical between Jesus' public ministry and their march to Jerusalem to celebrate the feast of the Passover for the last time.

Notes

[1] Ken Garfield, "Myers Park Presbyterian Pastor Quits," *Charlotte Observer* (Charlotte NC) 24 May 1995, PIC.

[2] Rodney Clapp, "Eugene Peterson: A Monk Out of Habit," *Christianity Today* 31/6 (3 April 1987): 24-25.

[3] Garfield.

Resources

US Campgrounds

Hodgson, Michael. *America's Secret Recreation Areas.* Santa Rosa: Foghorn Press, 1995.

Smith, Mary Helen and Shuford. *Camp the US for $5.00 or Less.* Old Saybrook CT: The Globe Press, 1994.

Sutherland, Laura, and Valerie Wolf Deutsch. *The Best Bargain Family Vacations in the USA.* New York: St. Martin's Press, 1997.

National Parks Ministry

2222 E. 49th St.
New York NY 10017
212-758-3450

Cruise Line Chaplaincy

Costa Cruise Lines
Attn: Jim diAmico
80 SW 8th St.
Miami FL 33130
800-462-6782

Cunard Lines, Ltd.
Attn: Pat Higgins
6100 Blue Lagoon Dr.
Suite 400
Miami FL 33126
305-463-3883

Lectures International
Attn: Helen Kelly
PO Box 35446
Tucson AZ 85740
206-281-3535

Norwegian Cruise Lines
Attn: Peter Grant
7665 Corporate Center Dr.
Miami FL 33126
1-800-327-7030

Posh Talks
PO Box 5417
Palm Springs CA 92263
760-323-3205

Premier Cruise Lines
Attn: A. Grier
900 South American Way
Miami FL 33132
305-358-5122
800-327-7113

Seabourn Cruise Lines
55 Francisco St.
Suite 710
San Francisco CA 94133
800-929-9595

A Covenant for Ministry: Pastor and People Together

Barrett Smith, D.Min.

"He leads me in right paths for his name's sake."

The relationship between minister and parish, like marriage, is blessed by God to be fruitful. This chapter proceeds on the assumption taken from family systems theory that marriage partners are generally "equally yoked." Rather than being destructive or a sign of failure, conflict between minister and parish is an opportunity for growth. Both may benefit from the conflicts and struggles that inevitably arise in relationships that really matter. Growing in the yoke is analogous to staying in the marriage and becoming more fully alive. It can be a win-win situation. Commitment to work through problems rather than leave a situation can be a turning point.

As in marriage, what persons (and pastors and churches) do *before* they become "married" has a great deal to do with how subsequent conflict will be handled. As the phrase from the 23rd Psalm suggests, the spiritual context of the relationship is foundational. To the extent that both pastor and people appreciate this and keep it foremost, they are able to move away from unrealistic expectations and rigid positions, which are the sources of many conflicts in the church. Perfection in personality or performance are no longer expected. The pastor and people more readily depend upon God's spirit to permeate their lives and to open before them the path to true reconciliation.

There are several levels of conflict in a congregation's response to different approaches toward a solution. Clergy antagonists, a special group of persons who spend much of their energy causing unrest in a church, are dealt with in another chapter. The unifying thread for our consideration will be how conflict between the New Grace Church and Rev. Jackson (a composite case) becomes creative rather than destructive. We will review the steps they took and the resources they studied in developing the Covenant for Yoking in Ministry. This covenant is offered as a resource for pastors and congregations who may wish to follow their example.

Rev. Jackson saw that the time had come to deal with the problems that had developed between certain members of the congregation and himself. The delegation that presented their "very serious matters" on the previous Sunday was surprised when Rev. Jackson reminded them of the church's covenant for yoking themselves in ministry and immediately suggested, as their covenant provided, that they consult the covenant for directions in developing a plan for moving beyond these problems. Not all members of the congregation had adjusted to the new way of being in mutual ministry, which was instituted when Rev. Jackson came to the church fourteen months ago. In the past, similar situations were resolved—as they frequently are—by a change of pastoral leadership as soon as possible. The church's unwritten rule of conflict avoidance had been: "When in conflict, divorce." When Rev. Jackson became pastor of New Grace Church, however, both he and the congregation decided they wanted a better way.

How could a congregation like New Grace decide to stand together and face the problems that occur when other similar congregations follow the line of least resistance and allow the conflict either to divide the church or force the pastor to move? What factors contribute to the quality and duration of the pastor-congregation relationship? Prior to Rev. Jackson's becoming pastor of New Grace Church, months were spent in conversation. The Covenant for Ministry in this chapter is the result of the labors of Rev. Jackson and the church and now governs their work together.

A Covenant for Ministry

The idea of a covenant for ministry came in the second meeting that New Grace Church had with Rev. Jackson. The group began to sense that everyone present was trying to impress, putting the most positive spin on all matters, and in some ways being dishonest by saying what they thought the other "party" wanted to hear. It was at this session that the group had a new insight: "If we begin our relationship on this basis, it is doomed to failure in much the same way other relationships have been. Let's try a new approach." Once they were able to verbalize these new realizations, Rev. Jackson and members of the committee shared regrets they had about ways they had responded to previous difficulties. They confessed that they had not always been part of the solution to problems that occurred within their congregation and then discussed how these learnings might inform their desire to approach the pastorate of a new minister and a new church in a new way. At the close of that session the group decided to work out what they called a "Covenant for Ministry" between the congregation and minister. They closed the meeting with real excitement and strong anticipation for their future meetings.

One resource that informed and challenged their efforts in the early days was Loren Mead's book, *Critical Moments of Ministry: A Change of Pastors*. In it the author identifies seven steps that occur during the time of pastoral change:

(1) termination
(2) direction finding
(3) self-study
(4) search
(5) decision/negotiation
(6) installation
(7) start-up

According to Mead, "There are points in the life of a group at which it may be particularly open to doing some tasks that lead it on to the next stage of its life with greater openness and with higher potential for creativity. Just as crises or major events in the life of a human being often give an opportunity for moving into new ground, discovering new abilities, trying new behavior, the same is true for congregations I have known and worked with."[1]

The New Grace group discussed this concept in great detail. The committee members felt it described what they were feeling as well as experiences that had proved difficult in the past. Their openness to address real issues gave them the courage to take a leap of faith, to discover new abilities and try new behavior.

The Interim Period

Loren Mead suggests there is a rich period between what he describes as "termination" and "startup" when it is possible for a congregation to deal most creatively with major life themes. He describes five tasks[2] that open themselves up to attention at the time of a changing of pastors:

• coming to terms with history
• discovering a new identity
• allowing needed leadership change
• renewing denominational linkages
• commitment to new directions in ministry

The New Grace group began by considering the relationship itself. First, the group viewed the relationship between pastor and parish through the lens of the marriage covenant. As in marriage, conflict between the pastor and the congregation is inevitable at some point. In fact, it is to be expected as part of God's way of maturing people. Sometimes the two parties react to the possibility or the reality of conflict in much the same way as the young couple who responded with surprise and discomfort when the minister asked them when they thought they would have their first fight and what issue the fight would concern. Congregations, like married couples, tend to deny or ignore conflict, hoping that it is not real and if it is, that it will just go away on its own. On such occasions one involved in the conflict will flee, whereas another will dig in and prepare for the fight. Almost always the idea that good might come from creative conflict is missed, and an opportunity for growth of both parties and the marriage itself is missed.

If marriage is blessed by God to be fruitful, could we assume that the covenant between a pastor and a congregation could receive the same blessing from God? It might be helpful at this point to review the pertinent facts relating to the case of Rev. Jackson and New Grace church.

Rev. Jackson is 48 years old and has served three other congregations since finishing seminary 23 years ago. New Grace Church is located in a midsized county seat town. There are 750 resident members and, in addition to the pastor, has a staff composed of a full-time secretary and two part-time program staff persons: a youth director and a choir director/organist. The secretary was hired by the former pastor six months before his departure. The choir director/ organist has been on staff for seven years, the youth director for 18 months.

After several visits from the pulpit committee of the New Grace Church, several different working sessions, and a final "contract signing" session, Rev. Jackson agreed to accept the church's call to be its pastor. Several months later, after moving in and adjusting to the new parish, a thoughtful and elaborate service of installation was carried out by the congregation, to which all churches in town were invited. During the early months Rev. Jackson spent a great deal of time getting acquainted with the people, the place, and the programs of the congregation and community. Informal sessions with leaders of the congregation and "coffees" for all members at his home helped to forge a bond between the pastor and individual persons. In addition, Rev. Jackson came to know other pastors in town and responded to invitations from civic clubs, schools, and community agencies to perform certain "ministerial" tasks. It was an exciting fourteen months for pastor and people alike, informally referred to as the "honeymoon period"—the time before the real tests begin.

One Sunday morning in Rev. Jackson's fifteenth month at New Grace Church, as final preparations were being made for the morning worship service, three members of the congregation appeared at the study door. Knocking at the closed door, they asked for a few minutes of Rev. Jackson's time to discuss some "very serious matters." Rev. Jackson explained that this was a bad time since the worship service was about to begin. After a brief discussion, a time later that afternoon was agreed upon. The delegation, somewhat put off, left. That afternoon, the group of three, which had expanded to seven, met with Rev. Jackson. The very serious matters they shared with the pastor were these:

- Some of the people are concerned that you are not in the church office in the mornings. "You need to be there and available in case the people need you."

- Some members believe the youth director is allowing the youth to have meetings in the church parlor, and that room is always locked! "Their concern is that you are not supervising the youth director closely enough."

- The biggest concern expressed by many members is that "you spend too much time visiting prospective members and in the jail, and not enough time visiting the long-time, faithful members. You know these people do not pay anything, and the church will really be in trouble if our regular members quit paying."

Principles of Healthy Relationships

In view of the Covenant for Ministry established when Rev. Jackson accepted the church's call, we might assume that New Grace Church has a better than average chance of dealing creatively with these "very serious matters" and growing in the process. This pastor and congregation appear to have learned several key principles of a healthy marriage relationship:

- Conflict in relationships is normal.
- We have more conflict with those we love most deeply.
- Relationships are strengthened when conflict is acknowledged and faced openly and honestly.

In establishing their covenant fourteen months earlier, the committee considered another concept that expands on the marriage theme. The relationship between pastor and parish could be likened to a yoke whereby pastor and people are bound together in a kind of crucible that "tests" the relationship. If the parties remain engaged through the conflict, the heat generated brings something altogether new into being—a deeper trust and greater intimacy. Marriage, at its best, is an equal yoking of partners where the relationship is strengthened by the hard work of communication and caring to the end that both partners are fulfilled. In biblical times a yoke united two animals in a common task. Jesus beckoned to his disciples:

> Come to me, all you that are weary and are carrying heavy burdens, and I will give you rest. Take my yoke upon you, and learn from me; for I am gentle and humble in heart, and you will find rest for your souls. For my yoke is easy, and my burden is light. (Matt 11:28-30)

The relationship among pastor, people, and God can be viewed as a yoke that unites them in a common task. Do pastors and congregations today experience the kind of holy alliance that enables them to work together toward the common goals of ministry? Or are they distracted by the many issues that seem to cause conflict between pastor and congregation? Where is God in the mix?

The yoking of a person and his/her ministry is a fragile thing. An axiom used in business says that job satisfaction leads to longevity in the job, and job satisfaction is best achieved by hiring the right person for the right job. Could this same axiom be applied to the relationship between a congregation and pastor? How can this yoking be achieved successfully, given the unique nature of the church?

Equally Yoked

Rev. Jackson and the laypersons from New Grace Church discussed what it means for a pastor and parish to be "equally yoked" and growing together. They listed some possibilities:

• similar views of the nature and mission of the church
• commitment to learning and growing together
• willingness to engage one another in authentic and honest dialogue
• clear expectations openly shared and negotiated
• reliance upon the Shepherd to provide and protect

It was their view that the Shepherd provides and protects because: Sheep can't do it alone, sheep need protection, sheep live in a hostile environment, and that's just what a shepherd does. What factors contributed to their desire for a better way? How were they able to convert this dream into a covenant that would govern their common tasks of being the church?

Members of the New Grace committee approached their work in the belief that too much energy is expended by the church in dealing with conflict after the fact. They had witnessed some churches seriously working through difficulty and calling on outside consultants or mediators to help them grow from the experience. They could name other churches or pastors, however, who decided to get a "divorce" rather than work through the conflict. What factors contribute to a pastor's or a congregation's decision?

One factor the committee identified was the way pastor and people view the pastor's call. In a talk-back sermon on the priesthood of all believers, a young minister made this statement. "I cannot be the 'good' man for this community. I am responsible before God for my own life and actions, and each of you is, too." During the talk-back segment, one extremely upset person responded by saying she expected the minister to be better than anyone else in the community, that she was appalled to hear him speak like that for, after all, "Isn't that what ministers are supposed to be?" This woman was concerned with the vocation of the minister. She perceived that a pastor had a special calling from and relationship with God and that by having a close relationship with the pastor, *she* would be closer to God. She interpreted his remarks to mean that he saw the ministry as a profession, not a calling or vocation. She was not willing to consider the notion that, in terms of duty and devotion to God, there might be no difference between the ministry and "secular" jobs. Lyle Schaller brought this issue into sharper focus when he said:

> The greater the emphasis on the parish ministry as a profession, the greater the chance that the people will seek a person who conveys a sense of being called to a vocation. (This is another reason why it is harder to be a pastor today than it was thirty years ago. In the 1950s nearly everyone agreed the parish ministry was a vocation. Today one group contends it is a profession while most of the church members still believe it to be a Christian vocation).[3]

Vocation or Profession?

The New Grace group spent a great deal of time discussing the issue of the pastorate as a vocation or profession. They recalled several ministers and congregations they had known that had approached this issue from different perspectives. They dealt with much that was written on the subject, including these two opposing views:

• "My vocation is not the way I earn my living but my willingness to use my life's energies and talents to make a difference in the world. Since I am a person of faith, I believe that I do not really need as many 'things' as I think I do, and that to live in community means to share my wealth with others. I do have a responsibility to be creative and productive, but not to the extent that I exploit anyone else or any other culture to obtain my desires. I want to join with others in bringing peace and justice in the world."

• "As I map out my career path, it is very important for me to negotiate, on an annual basis, the most lucrative compensation package possible. I owe it to myself for my long years of preparation and experience in my field, and to my family who makes sacrifices every day for me to advance in my profession. Also, I've learned that if I do not look after myself, no one else will. After all, everyone is in this game for himself or herself above all else."

What factors might contribute to a minister's and congregation's view of vocation? Is there any difference between the calling of a minister and that of a layperson? Does one's culture and political system contribute to the way ministry is lived? How does one live the simple life when one's society and even one's religious denomination values the "fruits" that are delivered by a vigorous economic system?

To aid them in exploring the question of vocation, the New Grace group turned to a characterization of vocation put forward by James Fowler:

Vocation is the response a person makes with his or her total self to the address of God and to the calling to partnership. The shaping of vocation as total response of the self to the address of God involves the orchestration of our leisure, our relationships, our work, our private life, our public life, and of the resources we steward, so as to put it all at the disposal of God's purposes in the services of God and the neighbor.[4]

This rather theoretical understanding of vocation took on a more human face in the delightful story from Carlyle Marney related by Fowler. Daisy was a wonderful Jersey cow owned by the Marney family. She gave rivers of milk that supplied the Presbyterian manse, the Methodist parsonage, and four gallons of milk per day for the Marneys. This ability to give so much milk also put Daisy in deep trouble when she calved. She suffered from mastitis from which she would die except for Mr. Adams' vocation:

> President of our small town bank, he lived just across the alley in a wide, low house. Four A.M.: new calf in the stall; Daisy down on her knees; Mr. Adams with a bicycle pump and ointments and hot water under Daisy's big belly; my father with Daisy's tail over his shoulder, straining to keep her hind quarters from going down. While an amateur veterinarian, bank president, Presbyterian elder, neighbor, father pumped and oiled and soothed Daisy into production for another season. This is vocation![5] . . .
>
> But who is Mr. Adams? Was he a neighbor, elder on a Christian mission, banker serving a very modest customer, or a cattleloving veterinarian with a sympathy for a hurting beast whose name came from the side of a churn? Answer: He was all of these at once. But in the arrangement of the scenery of his life's drama, he was living out his identity, using the special gifts, interests, experiences that gave him a role as a means of relation. And his work, his energy in relation, were all serving a proper relational end. The term for the wholerole, work, proper end, is vocation. And from which of the roles and ends is his identity derived? Answer: From none of them. He is all of them at once.[6]

Authority and Leadership

The New Grace committee discussed two related factors that contribute to a pastor's and a congregation's decision about conflict resolution: authority and leadership. Jackson Carroll points out that because of broad social and cultural changes that have occurred over many years, the authority and leadership of the clergy have been negatively affected. He cites the following factors:[7]

• the questioning of fundamental assumptions about God
• the marginalization of the church
• dependence upon volunteerism in the work of the church
• clergy emphasis on shared ministry with laity

In a discussion about the source of authority for ministry, Carroll further focuses on two penultimate bases of clergy authority: "clergy as representatives of the sacred and the clergyperson's specialized knowledge and expertise."[8]

For Carroll, the pastor interprets the power of God and points to the importance of some conception of the sacred, whether in terms of a transcendent God or more modestly as a set of core values and beliefs about an organization and its purpose. This is the ultimate basis of authority within a particular group. The leader is granted authority to lead because she or he is believed to protect, interpret, and represent the group's core values and beliefs and to contribute to their realization. People grant authority to scripture and the church's tradition(s) and to those who interpret them—because they believe, in the last analysis, that these authorities are grounded in God and God's purposes for the world.[9]

Rev. Jackson and members of the committee were struck by the fact that what Carroll is saying had been under the surface in much of their previous experience, but had never really surfaced. They came to understand that this one issue was the source of much conflict they had experienced between the pastor and the congregation. They decided to include a strategy for dealing creatively with this issue in their Covenant for Ministry.

The New Grace committee was beginning to realize that the relationship between a pastor and a congregation is a fragile thing. How the two come together is interpreted by some as preordained or "meant to be." For some, it is the result of hours, even years, of negotiation; for others, it is an appointment based on the appropriate salary levels and other intangible "gifts and graces." For others, it is a mix of preordination, negotiation, and appointment. Where one's church or ministry fits into this structure depends upon one's perception and one's denomination's method of yoking minister (or pastor) and congregation (or parish). We certainly do not want to think that the matching of the two is mere chance or that God is not involved in the process.

Over many decades various denominations, religions, and even sects have developed different approaches and theologies toward the role, uniqueness, and responsibilities of the church and of ministry. For some, there is a very low-key, informal arrangement; for others, an elaborate, formal system has evolved. Some believe that all persons are called to special ministries and that ministers merely point the way or help equip all the saints for ministry. Others believe that the calling to ministry is a special relationship between the person and God and that this relationship should be enhanced and even revered.

Much can be written toward the aim of bringing together the most appropriate congregation with the best suited minister. "An ounce of prevention . . ." is without a doubt best for both clergy and congregation. Sometimes congregations develop a profile of a minister. They describe desired qualities such as age, family situation, education/training, and experience in previous similar situations, only to discover later that the person they thought was their "ideal" was the wrong person. Likewise, ministers may mentally make their lists of the most desirable congregational situations, go for the one that seems logically to be the best match, only to find themselves miserably unhappy in a few months. How can this happen when both pastor and parish have worked so diligently to match their gifts and graces? On the other hand, why do some pastors and congregations "hit it off" from the start and have a long and fruitful relationship?

Taking a look at other denominations helped Rev. Jackson and the New Grace committee gain a new perspective on their denomination and a deeper appreciation for other traditions. They decided to include in their covenant an explicit way of relating more maturely to their denomination in the future.

At the next meeting one of the members excitedly requested time to share some insights she had gained from a book written especially for laypersons. She brought a copy of *What Every Church Member Should Know about Clergy* by Robert Kemper. She shared that, according to Kemper, the source of health in churches is trust and that if a church is to be healthy, it must discover and practice those things that increase trust between the pastor and the congregation. The main way to increase trust is the advancement of understanding. "What is not understood is menacing, too. But more positively, what is understood is trustworthy."[10]

These ideas were intriguing to the group members, who decided to take a closer look at this resource. Upon careful study, they realized that the process of understanding goes on forever and that pastors and laity must understand each other. In the process of seeking to understand one another, they must ask and seek to answer two elemental questions: Who are we, and what are we trying to accomplish together?

Next, the group centered around Kemper's assertion that there are certain false and erroneous signs and symbols of trust within the congregation, for example, peace and concord, prosperity and growth. The author points out that the presence of these conditions in a congregation does not necessarily mean that trust exists. It is likely that pastor and congregation have agreed to submerge their pursuit of trust and understanding in order to attend to more pressing demands. The author points out, however, that "the submersion is temporary. The processes of trustbuilding and the quest for understanding can lie dormant for some time, even years, but they will surface, clamoring for air, demanding attention."[11]

The study of this resource gave new energy to Rev. Jackson and the New Grace group. They sensed that they were being helped to confront issues that would serve them well in the future of their relationship. They struggled with some of Kemper's questions: Can the laity talk with one another openly and with respect? Can the laity accept differences and disagreements? Can conflicts be resolved through negotiation and reconciliation so losers do not feel like outcasts when they have lost?[12]

The group members decided to incorporate in their Covenant for Ministry Kemper's two signs of quality in pastor-parish relationships: creative coping and celebrative events. Statements with which the group resonated included:

• "Creative coping by churches is coming to grips with the realities of the situation in which churches find themselves. Much waste goes on in churches that wish they were something else other than what they are . . . Another place, another program, another minister, another . . . whatever, anything but what is, will save us . . . creative coping is more creative than it is coping. Quality pastor-parish relationships are those in which freshness, innovation, experimentation are not dirty words . . . We trust each other enough to try."[13]

• "Quality pastor-parish relationships are life-affirming. Pastor and parish are grateful to God for life itself and especially for life together . . . festival moments are occasions to express love and concern for one another. Church celebrative events are love and care for one another in the name of, and for the sake of, Christ. Even somber events such as a funeral, a farewell to a departing, beloved pastor are celebrative events; they lift up all of life in praise to God and thank God for mercies and grace through all of life."[14]

When the time comes to make a ministerial change, perhaps a minister and a congregation would do well to examine their readiness point, or where need meets experience. Instead of depending upon such objective factors as "SWM desires nonsmoking SWF . . ."—which might match perfectly—what about looking at the readiness level of each party? Like a minister, a church has its own struggles, life, and personality. Most churches have a reputation, as does a minister. Churches, too, have a readiness point. With total abandon, they must identify that readiness point when it is time to find a new minister. Churches must evaluate where they have been and where they need to go. Then they must identify their own resources to meet their needs. The place at which the readiness point of a congregation meets or matches the readiness point of the pastor can be the beginning of a fruitful relationship.

How does this proposal look in reality? A church of 150 members has for fifty years successfully ministered to a rural, conservative community and congregation. It has a rich history of tradition and treats all of its pastors with deference (any pastor's dream congregation). However, suddenly, within the last five years, the congregation has found itself being used and described as a "bedroom community" of a nearby city. New subdivisions are being built, and new people are moving in. Traditions are treated casually by newcomers, and many longstanding members are threatened. After the last pastor became a casualty of this changing situation, new ministerial leadership is now being sought. How does this church identify its readiness point? What minister's readiness point matches the church's and would make a perfect union?

The Yoke of Servanthood

Taking upon oneself the yoke of servanthood is difficult today. Four major factors influence the effectiveness of the yoking: economics, denominational polity, expectations, and demands.

Economics, translated into salary and benefits, become the primary focus for much of a pastor's work in the current congregation. With the benefits of the current work representing status and acceptance, pastors expend much energy in comparing their "package" with other pastors and positioning themselves to move up the economic ladder at the next opportunity. Therefore, we might ask: Does God place a pastor in the church s/he needs. Or is it the pastor's efforts to "use the system" for personal advantage? How can a pastor and a congregation commit themselves to a long-term relationship if the focus is on the "best deal" economically for both the pastor *and* the congregation? Coming to terms with this issue from a biblical and theological perspective offers a great deal of freedom for pastor and congregation alike.

Another factor that influences the effectiveness of the yoke between pastor and congregation is *denominational polity*. The methods of deploying pastors used by major denominations today can be grouped under three categories.[15] Churches in the first two categories call their pastors; churches in the third category appoint their pastors:

- *completely open*—Baptists; Church of God of Anderson, Indiana; Christian Church (Disciples of Christ)
- *restricted open*—Presbyterians, Episcopal, Church of the Nazarene, Reformed Church in America
  - *closed*—The United Methodist Church and other bodies with Methodist roots

Under the call system, each congregation, when a vacancy of pastoral leadership occurs, begins a search for a new pastor. In some situations, an interim pastor is secured to provide for preaching and other specified duties. A pulpit committee, empowered to represent the interests of the congregation, begins to interview candidates and hear them preach. Usually, only one or a few candidates is asked to preach before the congregation and respond to inquiries from the congregation. Through this careful selection process, the best possible pastor for the church is secured.

Under the appointive system, changes in pastoral leadership occur in several churches at the same time. A cabinet of peers considers the churches open for new pastoral leadership and the gifts and graces of the pastors seeking a position. Of major consideration is the salary level of each pastor and the compensation level of each congregation. Through a process of consultation with pastors and congregations, the bishop makes appointments for a period of one year at a time. A unique feature of this system is that every church always has a pastor and every pastor, in good standing, has a church (a guaranteed appointment).

A third factor that influences the quality of the yoking between pastor and congregation is *expectations* of each. Lyle Schaller, in his book, *The Pastor and the People,* offers a practical way for the pastor to share with the congregation his/her personal priorities and for the members to do the same. A very simple "game" can provide profound insights for all persons involved in a congregation's life. A pack of twelve cards, each with a different priority on the pastor's time, is distributed to members of the pastor-parish committee (or other leadership group in the church). After clarifying the issue so that everyone is responding to the same question (What are the priorities on the pastor's time; or what should be the priorities . . .), each person is asked to discard the four lowest priorities and then arrange the remaining cards in order of importance to him/her. (It is often helpful if the minister shares at the end of each round.) Then the participants discuss the similarities, differences, trends, and implications these learnings might have for the congregation. Next, the group looks at the discarded cards and asks some of the same questions. This process is a tool to stimulate creative and constructive discussion.[16]

The fourth factor that influences the quality of the yoking between pastor and people is the various *demands* placed upon them. The issue of demands is often "the straw that breaks the camel's back" with many congregations and pastors. Closely related to expectations, it is often not treated as such. By the time something becomes a "demand," a great deal of communication has already been lost. One minister reflected on the "demands" placed on him in this way: "I have learned in the parish that on any subject there is always someone who takes all points of view. It is impossible to please everyone or to make all sides happy. To take a stand on an issue and clearly state your reasoning (while acknowledging the opinions of others) serves you better in the long run than always riding the fence or having no opinion."

The main task of pastor and people is to be open to, yet seeking, the physical and spiritual resources the Shepherd provides. This involves taking time to "be still and remember . . ." and modeling one's life and ministry after the Shepherd. Could it also involve rejecting the temptation to allow the expectations/demands of the congregation/denomination to make one's work routine rather than a vocation?

Do we need a ritual for yoking pastor and people to one another, to a common task, and to God? How might this approach to a beginning ministry contribute to a long and fruitful relationship? What effect might it have when conflict situations arise? Is it possible that both pastor and people might continue in creative ministry for better or for worse? When should the yoke be broken or laid aside? Who decides and how?

How can a pastor and parish benefit from conflicts/struggles that arise? Growing in the yoke in the parish can be a turning point in the relationship between a pastor and a parish. This, however, may be more of an ideal than a reality in many situations. In the United Methodist Church, for example, the system guarantees every pastor an appointment and every church a pastor. Under this arrangement, many times the pastor and people operate out of the mind-set that "we don't have to confront the issue; we can just get a new pastor (or church)." Some churches and pastors never consider a long-term relationship that could endure with careful, intentional cultivation for many years because the "system" offers a remedy that is the easy way out. Another causality of this approach is the pastor's family members who are traumatized due to no fault of their own. At times, pastors become scapegoats because they are convenient targets when the parish (or a vocal segment of the parish) is unable or unwilling to identify and honestly confront the issue(s) that divides the pastor and the parish. Sometimes ministers leave the church before being asked to leave or instead of giving the energy necessary to resolve conflicts in the parish. Could this be the result of unequal or inadequate yoking from the very beginning?

Is it possible that a pastor's ability or willingness to stay rather than flee is related to the original call, or personality, or the way he/she deals with conflict? Do pastors who have a "mentor" fall into the trap of being disillusioned when they experience the realities of the parish? Do churches develop a habit or preferred way of relating to pastors regardless of who the pastor is? How can these cycles be broken or changed?

Resolving Conflict

Several factors contribute to the effective yoking of the minister and the people. Among these are:

- similar biblical and theological understanding of the church and ministry (lay and professional)
- commitment, by pastor and people, to a long-term relationship
- intentional occasions for trust-building early in the relationship
- sharing expectations and agreeing on roles/responsibilities all parties will embrace
- sharing of dreams, goals, and priorities for church's ministry
- structure for planning, implementing, and evaluating: (a) ministries of the church and (b) their work together
- a commitment to honestly and authentically engage one another for the solution of problems rather than breaking communication:

Using the "Problem Severity Scale" (p. 89) can help resolve conflict between the pastor and member(s) of the congregation. The persons for whom the problem exists should respond to the following questions under each category and then pinpoint the severity of the problem based on a scale of 1-10:

Questions

Mild
• Did the act show the pastor's/member's absentmindedness or over-extended schedule?
• Did the act disappoint the pastor/member?
• Was the act unintentional?

Moderate
• Did the act show the pastor's/member's disregard for another's feelings?
• Did the act make the pastor/member angry?
• Was the act intentional?

Severe
• Did the act compromise the pastor's/member's integrity/competence?
• Did the act cause the pastor/member to lose trust in one another's leadership?
• Was the act against the law or morally questionable?

0	5	10
Mild	Moderate	Severe

Responses

Mild
• Sit down, face to face to discuss problem.
• Listen attentively and repeat what you have heard; don't blame.
• Agree on a solution, compromising if necessary, and move on.

Moderate
• The pastor/congregation liaison committee identifies the problem, hears from all sides, and comes to a reasonable solution for all parties.
• Share, as appropriate, with the congregation.
• Establish a time frame for coming to a solution and a method for evaluating progress toward the goal.

Severe
- Inform the congregation of the basic facts surrounding the problem and of the specifics steps that are being taken, and by whom, to solve the problem.
- Secure an outside resource (mediator, counselor, etc.) to work out a solution to the problem.
- Develop a plan to involve the entire congregation in claiming ownership in the agreement reached and committing themselves to the hard work required in the weeks ahead.

Simply put, the key to resolving conflict is this: Act when the problem first appears. Don't wait, thinking it will go away or solve itself—it won't!

Printed on page 91 is the result of long and diligent work by a pastor and a group of lay leaders from our composite congregation. Whether this congregation is typical or very unusual could be a matter of debate, possibly depending upon one's previous experience in a congregation. The important matters to remember, however, are that with a desire for authentic relationships and an emphasis on the spiritual nature and mission of the church, a group of thoughtful, committed, and self-assured persons can decide to yoke themselves equally in ministry. Their willingness to take another's point of view, to listen with the heart as well as the head, to work intentionally at developing genuine caring and trust, and their openness to being held accountable for their life and work in the congregation can make all the difference. It is important, too, to remember that, just as in marriage, the relationship between pastor and people is always growing, changing, and facing new challenges of communication, conflict resolution, and mutual fulfillment. If pastor and people rely upon the goodwill generated in their authentic and honest sharing of themselves and the power of God's spirit to bless their covenant, they will truly be led in right paths for His name's sake.

Covenant for Yoking in Ministry
New Grace Church

Because it is our desire to establish a working relationship that calls for the greatest possible creativity, to use the best talents of pastor and people alike, and to relate to one another with honesty and integrity, we agree to the following guidelines for our common life together:

We recognize the vocation of all Christians to live in the service of God and of God's children. We affirm that because of special training and ordination by the denomination, our pastor will perform duties of word and sacrament and give spiritual direction to our congregation. We further affirm that each lay person will, after careful consideration of his/her gifts and graces, be in significant service of God through the church.

As we begin our work together, we do so expecting a longterm relationship and commit ourselves to work toward that end.

We affirm the importance of trust in the relationship between pastor and people. We will intentionally plan and carry out occasions for building trust between the pastor and church members early in the relationship. Building trust and working to understand one another will be constant tasks of this congregation and this pastor.

Because it is our desire that every person, regardless of age or station, related to our congregation have ownership in our mission and know that he/she has a place in our fellowship, we will have periodic celebrative events (in addition to regular, common events held throughout the church year). We will observe longstanding traditions and establish new ones.

Because of an increasing knowledge of and appreciation for our denominational tradition, we pledge ourselves to cultivate closer ties between our church and our denomination.

We pledge ourselves to evaluate on an annual basis our ministry, mission, and our working together. We will give our best efforts in achieving the goals of our congregation and will be willingly held accountable for the part of God's work for which we are responsible.

We commit ourselves to honestly and authentically engage one another for the solution of problems rather than break off communication. We will use the Problem Severity Scale to help us solve our problems and grow from them. We designate our Pastor-Parish Committee to meet regularly to keep lines of communication open between pastor and congregation, and to act immediately deal to with conflicts when they arise.

Whenever pastor or congregation wishes to explore a change of pastoral leadership, we commit ourselves to the highest level of communication when arriving at the decision that is best for all parties. We will celebrate the learning and growth from this unique relationship when it ends.

Notes

[1] Loren B. Mead, *Critical Moment of Ministry: A Change of Pastors* (Washington DC: The Alban Institute, 1988) 37.

[2] Ibid., 36-50.

[3] Lyle E. Schaller, *It's A Different World* (Nashville: Abingdon, 1987) 207.

[4] James W. Fowler, *Becoming Adult, Becoming Christian* (San Francisco: Harper & Row, 1984) 95.

[5] Ibid., 95-96.

[6] Ibid., 96.

[7] Jackson W. Carroll, *As One with Authority* (Louisville KY: Westminster/ John Knox, 1991) 19.

[8] Ibid., 9-10.

[9] Ibid., 43.

[10] Robert G. Kemper, *What Every Church Member Should Know about Clergy* (New York: The Pilgrim Press, 1985) 154-59.

[11] Ibid., 157-58.

[12] Ibid., 158.

[13] Ibid.

[14] Ibid., 159.

[15] Jackson W. Carroll and Robert L. Wilson, *Too Many Pastors?* (New York: The Pilgrim Press, 1980) 33-35.

[16] Lyle E. Schaller, *The Pastor and the People* (Nashville: Abingdon, 1986).

Suggested Readings

Biles, Daniel V. *Pursuing Excellence in Ministry.* New York: The Alban Institute, 1988. Results of interviews with pastors and laity from four dozen highly recommended Lutheran churches. Integration of theological perspectives with understanding of the Foundations on Excellence in the church: (1) mission, (2) leadership, (3) lay commitment and ownership.

Carroll, Jackson W., Carl S. Dudley, and William McKinney. *Handbook For Congregational Studies*. Nashville: Abingdon Press, 1986. A practical guide for a congregational self-study, including an excellent Parish Profile Inventory, from three authors with extensive and varied experience relating to many congregations at different stages.

Friedman, Edwin H. *Generation to Generation: Family Process in Church and Synagogue*. New York: Guilford Press, 1985. Application of the concepts of family systems therapy to the emotional life of pastors and congregations.

Oswald, Roy M. and Robert E. Friedrich, Jr. *Discerning Your Congregation's Future: A Strategic and Spiritual Approach*. New York: The Alban Institute, 1996. A call to prayer for discernment and a systematic approach to a congregation's discerning its future. Includes appendices with valuable resources: Guidelines for Fasting; A Congregational Health Inventory; Centering Prayer; How To Minister Effectively in Family, Pastoral, Program, and Corporate-Sized Churches.

Taylor, Barbara Brown. *The Preaching Life*. Boston: Cowley Publications, 1993. Thought-provoking and inspiring sermons and reflections on the tasks of the pastor, relationships in the congregation, understanding of call, vocation, and imagination.

Living in the Fishbowl

Ron King, Ph.D.

"Even though I walk through the darkest valley,
I fear no evil; for you are with me."

The peculiar stresses on the family life of clergy are well known: being constantly on-call, interrupted vacations, calling on the spouse as "free labor," spouses having no minister, etc. This chapter identifies the major stressors of clergy life and offers practical methods for dealing with them effectively in a context of honoring the whole body of Christ.

Janice can't believe her ears. Chris isn't coming home tonight. His secretary telephoned and told her that Chris was called to the hospital for an emergency and doesn't know when he will be able to leave. Janice knows that doctors can't leave the hospital in an emergency, but since when can the pastor not leave? Besides, it is their fifth wedding anniversary, and they have planned a special evening together. This is the last time she will live this way. As she packs her suitcases, Janice can't believe her feelings. She loves the people in the congregation, but Chris acts like he is married to the church but occasionally sleeps with her. She knows exactly how single parents in the church feel. She can never count on her husband for anything. There is always a committee meeting, a church prospect to visit, a pastoral care emergency, or something. He always has time for church, but never has time to be with her or the baby.

Janice's experience is the experience of numerous clergy spouses throughout congregations of America across all denominational lines. According to *Christianity Today*, between 1970 and 1990 the number of clergy divorces in the United States increased by 65%. This will not surprise most clergy couples, but it does perhaps surprise the laity.

The difficulties that clergy couples experience are similar to the difficulties other couples in society face. However, these stressors and conflicts are intensified by the expectations clergy couples have of themselves and the expectations their congregations have for them. Clergy marriages and families are judged by a higher set of standards than the rest of society. In a survey conducted among clergy couples by David and Vera Mace in the late 1970s (no female clergy and clergy husbands were included in the survey), 85% of pastors and 59% of clergy wives listed the number one disadvantage of being a clergy couple was that their marriage was expected to be a model of perfection.[1] Some may suggest this expectation has changed in the past two decades, but others would disagree.

The Congregation's Expectations

In the mid-1990s, as part of an experiment, the zoo in Copenhagen, Denmark, placed a human couple in a Plexiglas cage as one of its exhibits to help visitors think about their ties to nature.[2] Clergy couples could tell the Copenhagen couple much about being on display for others. Life in a cage or goldfishbowl is a reality for clergy families. Many congregations view ministers and their families as not only "representing" them, but also as "belonging" to them. The congregation places realistic and unrealistic expectations on clergy families.

Clergy families may feel at times as though they are to be superhuman and perfect models of individual and family conduct. Clergy families respond to these demands and expectations in a variety of ways. Frequently the response of the clergy and the response of the spouse are at odds, and the resulting tension contributes to marital and family conflict and turmoil that multiplies the stress on the family. At no time is this more evident in clergy families than during the preschool and teen years.

Clergy families with children in these two age groups experience tremendous tension between the demands of church and the demands of the family. All too often ministers' families may feel they are expected to live and rear children in a different dimension of space and time than other persons.

The church had called Diane and Charles less than a year ago. Charles was the associate pastor in charge of the youth and music programs. The rapidly growing congregation had doubled in size over the past three years due to the church's location. The youth program was booming, and Charles felt conflicted trying to balance the demands of the expanding youth program with the responsibilities of the music program. Several of the founding members of the congregation were very active in the adult choir. They were struggling with all of the changes going on in the congregation and the rapid expansion of the programs due to the increased number of new families joining the church.

Two of the retired families invited Charles and his family to dinner after the Sunday services to discuss their concerns. Charles, Diane, Elizabeth (age 3), and John (10 months) all joined the four mature adults at the local restaurant for a "relaxing" lunch after the two morning services. Both children were fussing and whining before the meal was finished because the baby was ready for his nap and the preschooler was out of her routine. As the adults tried to finish their dessert and share in "adult" conversation, the preschooler began to act out, seeking attention from her parents. The choir members began to wonder why the associate pastor and his wife could not better "control" their children. The meal ended with everyone feeling frustrated, and the adults beginning to wonder if Charles was really the person to serve their congregation.

Family routines and needs of the preschoolers may often conflict with the social expectations placed on clergy families by members of the congregation. The simple function of being a guest for a meal can become a physical and spiritually exhausting experience for all members of the clergy family.

The teen years can be even more intense for the clergy family and their church. Many teenagers experience times of pulling back from active church participation or they attend neighboring congregations as a normal part of gaining some distance from their parents and family. Clergy teens may become the subject of criticism or judgment if they miss church or a youth activity. Frequently they are expected to participate 100% of the time, and their absence is seen to reflect on their minister parent in the minds of some members.

Members and clergy alike are aware that Paul's letter to Timothy admonishes those who serve the church to be faithful in their marriages and "manage their children and their households well" (1 Tim 3:12). The definition of "control" for the clergy family may have a somewhat different interpretation than it does for other "normal" families. In numerous denominations, what was true in previous generations continues to be the guideline: There is one standard of expectations for the clergy family and another for the laity.

Lloyd Rediger observes that sometimes congregations injure their ministers by placing unrealistic expectations on them. Some congregations even contain what Rediger calls "clergy killers." These are often parishioners who have been wounded by the church or a previous pastor and assume the role of making the minister's life as miserable as possible. Certainly not every church includes this type of person, but more than a few congregations do. The church often contributes to the destruction of this experience by allowing the minister and his/her family to suffer these scathing attacks alone.[3]

The expectations placed on clergy may be subtle or not so subtle, and they come from everyone in the congregation. As authority figures, clergy often become parental substitutes onto whom parishioners project unresolved anger or needs related to their parents. In incidents where ministers have met significant pastoral care needs during times of personal and family crises, they are experienced as caring, nurturing figures. The families to whom they have ministered may develop an idealistic view of their pastor and often become the clergy's most ardent supporters. Pastors who are not there to minister in a timely manner during times of personal and family crisis will experience a distancing and judging from their parishioners. Expectations run high for clergy, clergy marriages, and clergy families. The fishbowl is a reality.

Self-Expectations

The congregation's expectations are complicated by the clergy's expectations of themselves. Numerous clergy and clergy couples place unrealistic expectations on themselves for their lives and ministries.

Many clergy and their spouses can be characterized as idealistic, perfectionistic, approval seekers. They seek to serve and accommodate. While these traits contribute well to their servanthood, they may wreak havoc on family dynamics.

Clergy couples may become so involved in their "church" work and their "commitment" to ministry that they do not make or take the time required for their own personal, marital, and family lives. Clergy members may be so enamored with the attention, praise, and feelings of accomplishment they experience in their ministry that they invest minimally in theirr relationship with their spouse. The "success" of ministry becomes addictive, and there is never enough time to do all that needs to be done. So as congregational expectations continue to grow, the clergy's expectations of themselves continue to expand. This can lead to a "workaholic" perspective that becomes destructive for the clergy, family, and congregation.

Many clergy members "need to be needed," which unfortunately has contributed to their tremendous success as ministers and abysmal failure as spouses or parents. The balancing act is extremely difficult, and God's strength and spirit are essential to becoming the person able to meet all of the expectations.

The young pastor, John Mims, received the call as he was shaving. The chief of police, a member of his congregation, wanted him to come to Jim and Claire's home as soon as possible. He told the pastor that Jim, age fifty, had suffered a massive heart attack and died while Claire administered CPR. Jim and Claire were very active parishioners. In fact, Claire had served on the search committee that had called John to the church. He felt very close to Jim and Claire. They had celebrated birthdays together over the years. The police and emergency vehicles were parked in the drive when he arrived. As John rushed up the steps, he saw Jim's body being loaded into the ambulance. His mind flooded with emotions, but he pushed them away. He entered the home, and Claire met him in the foyer. She grabbed him and cried uncontrollably as she said, "John, John, we celebrated our twenty-ninth anniversary last night and now this. Why did God do this? How could this happen?"

John was overwhelmed with feelings of grief and pain as he heard himself speaking, but he wasn't sure of what he was saying. Two hours later after Claire had told everyone coming in the door what she had told him, he left to return to his office at the church. Family and church members were there for Claire, and he felt okay about leaving.

Upon entering the office, his secretary was anxious to know the details because calls were already coming in. She also had more bad news for him. Mr. Lewis, an elderly member of the congregation who had been hospitalized for several days, had passed away last evening in his sleep. The funeral was scheduled for tomorrow. Performing both funerals that week, John also ministered to the Carsons and their fourteen-year-old daughter who received a definitive diagnosis on Friday that she had leukemia and needed immediate treatment. The prognosis was not good.

Upon arriving home that evening, John was distant and withdrawn from his family. His children wondered what they had done to make Dad so upset. His wife felt isolated and cut off from her husband. She was worried about their future. John's self-expectations, his compound grief experiences, and his desire to please others combined to create an extremely stressful experience for his family that may be repeated frequently throughout his ministry.

For effectiveness in ministry, ministers must develop a realistic perspective on self-expectations. The work of ministry will frequently feel overwhelming; therefore, ministers must find ways to cope constructively with the demands and opportunities.

Time Expectations

The time demands experienced by clergy families are unique. Few professional families in America experience less control of their time schedule than the pastor's family. Many clergy report evening work five to seven nights a week. One or two evenings are often dedicated to visitation of church members or congregational prospects because this is when the other families are home together. Another evening may be dedicated to a midweek prayer service, while still another one or two is dedicated to church board, church committees, or organizational community meetings. Throw in the Sunday School class evening meetings, socials, wedding rehearsals, weddings, and Sunday evening worship services, and most nights will find the clergy somewhere other than at home with their families.

Reverend Edwards could not wait for Friday. It had been one of those weeks. In addition to the Wednesday night prayer service he conducted, he had averaged two church meetings every day for the past two weeks. This week he had also attended four community meetings and was the featured speaker for two of them. He had spent three afternoons and one evening at the hospital. He was concerned about the two youth who had been in an automobile accident. Fortunately, both would live, although their condition had been critical for two days. He had forgotten how exhausting those long nights at the hospital could be. He had not been able to catch up on his sleep, and he was extremely tired. He hoped he could sleep late Saturday morning. Sundays were long days.

When he arrived home, his wife asked him if he needed a shirt ironed for the wedding rehearsal and dinner that evening. He had forgotten all about the wedding rehearsal. His sermons were barely ready for Sunday, and now he remembered the Friday night wedding rehearsal and dinner and Saturday afternoon wedding. He had hoped to use most of Saturday for background reading on the new Sunday evening teaching series he was beginning. He could not remember a time when he felt so emotionally and spiritually depleted. He loved this church and his ministry, but he sure felt out of control of his life at the moment. He wondered when and if he would ever feel in control again.

The time schedule for clergy of being on call 24 hours a day, 365 days a year becomes very stressful at times. Few professionals in modern-day society experience as constant a demand in this area as clergy. Physicians now share being on call with their colleagues and have times scheduled where they are not available to their patients. Clergy have not yet developed this practice. The stressors of being on call, available for any and all pastoral care emergencies, frequently exact a costly toll on clergy families. More than a few clergy family vacations have been affected by a telephone call requesting the pastor to return to the church to minister to a family in crisis, which frequently involves a death or impending death.

Many congregations have such a sense of "ownership" of their pastor and pastor's family that they feel free to call the ministers at home late in the evenings to ask simple questions that could easily have been managed the following day during "normal" hours. This sense of entitlement expressed by these actions of some church members is not found in many other professional relationships. Numerous clergy couples report the heavy schedule demands placed on them by the church as a major stress on their marriages and families. Time alone on a weekly, monthly, and annual basis as a couple or family without the demands of the church interfering is a tremendous need for clergy families.

Spousal Expectations

Congregational demands often extend to clergy spouses, who are still expected by some churches to serve as assistant pastors. These expectations are perhaps not as great as they were in previous generations, but they are implicit in numerous congregations. The role of the spouse as a youth leader, Sunday School teacher, church host or hostess is an expectation on the part of numerous congregations and members.

Until the last half of the twentieth century, most clergy spouses did not work outside the home. After the children entered school, the spouse had time to lead prayer groups, mission studies, special programs, and teach Sunday School classes. During this same time period few women served as senior ministers, and congregations were not dealing with male spouses of clergy.

In today's fast-paced, two-career families, clergy spouses—male or female—may be overextended, physically tired, and emotionally exhausted at the end of the work day or the work week. Whenever congregation members need a break, they may skip a Wednesday night church supper or sleep in on Sunday morning. Clergy spouses are not often permitted this luxury. Although the expectations are changing and the pressure may not be as intense for male spouses, many congregation members continue to hold very high standards for church participation for clergy spouses. This dynamic may often intensify the level of tension between the clergy and spouse and create an atmosphere where guilt, not joy, becomes the motivation of church activities.

Clergy Care

The life of the clergy family can be very rewarding and very demanding at the same time. Realistic and unrealistic expectations are continually being placed on ministers and their families as the church moves into the twenty-first century. The clergy and clergy family called by God to serve the church must be as intentional in their self-care, marital care, and family care as they are in their ministries to the congregations. Caring for personal and family needs in the midst of caring for everyone else's needs is not optional for clergy and their family members; it is as essential as prayer and eating. Humans are created for spiritual and physical exercise on a daily basis. Marital and family relationships need daily contact as well.

Dealing with the constancy of demands and expectations of the church and society means the clergy couple and clergy families must give consistent attention to maintaining their balance and perspective on life and ministry. The realities of awareness, balance, and connection constitute the ABCs of clergy family care and can help clergy and their families flourish in the ebb and flow of daily life and ministry.

Awareness
The first essential is for clergy and clergy spouses to develop an awareness of their spiritual, emotional, and relational needs. This awareness can best be attended to by developing and maintaining daily personal time for quiet reflection and prayer. During times of particular stress, it could be helpful to ask questions such as "How do I feel right now?" and "What are my energy levels?" An awareness of spiritual and emotional energy levels is critical. The spirit can become depleted just as the body becomes depleted without adequate nourishment, exercise, and physical care. A regular time of reflection and prayer can replenish the spirit and enhance self-awareness.

Jesus developed a pattern in his ministry that the Gospel writers consistently report. He regularly left the demands of the people following him daily and went away for a time of spiritual renewal and prayer. Clergy more often than not become so immersed in "ministry" that they fail to take the time to "go away" for periods of spiritual renewal and prayer.

Rev. Jimmy Cooke had a regular pattern that was respected and honored throughout his fifty-plus years of ministry. He went to the mountains one day a week for spiritual renewal and prayer. He had a regular spot just outside his town where he walked through nature, read, reflected, and prayed for one day each week. He credits God as using this pattern of weekly spiritual retreats to empower him personally and spiritually in his ministry. He had a long and fruitful ministry.

In addition to spiritual and emotional needs, pastors must maintain an awareness of the relational and family needs of their spouse, children, and other family members. Maintaining an awareness of the needs of those closest to the pastor can often be unintentionally overlooked when so many other needs are demanding attention.

An awareness of the relational and family needs can be facilitated by spending regular periods of time with spouses and family members. One way clergy can keep in regular contact with their spouse is by taking a brief walk together late in the afternoons or later in the evening. This walk and talk time will help each remain aware of the demands, stressors, and experiences of the other. The walk can also help relieve some of the built-up stress in the body.

Periods of constant ministry to persons experiencing trauma, loss, or grief can significantly impact the pastor's emotional and spiritual well-being. These feelings are frequently carried home and emotionally contaminate the spirit of the marriage and/or the family. Clergy can develop an awareness of their own grief reactions that result from their ministries to persons experiencing trauma and death. This awareness enables the clergy to be more effective caregivers. Without this awareness, the clergy ministry, marriage, and family are at greater risk.

In the frantic, overly hectic ministry of clergy, maintaining this sense of awareness is essential. The more intense the demands on personal and family time, the more critical it is to maintain a sense of personal, emotional, spiritual, and relational awareness.

Balance

Maintaining a sense of balance in ministry is the second essential element in the ABCs of clergy care. Work, rest, and play must be balanced for clergy and spouses. At times the idea of maintaining a balance seems impossible to clergy couples. One simple change that can help with the balancing act is for clergy couples to give themselves permission to schedule their time differently than the rest of the work world.

Ted gradually realized that he had less and less energy as the demands of the church continued to grow. He knew he needed more exercise. Having been an avid runner most of his life, he struggled to find a convenient time to run. He wanted to be with his family at breakfast since his daughter caught a 7:00 AM bus. He had meetings at the church late in the afternoon and many evenings. Over time he discovered that he could fit in time for his three-mile run earlier in the afternoon after hospital visitation. At first he felt guilty about not being at the office later in the afternoon, but he quickly realized that taking this time for exercise made him much more effective in his ministry. Clergy have more flexibility with their schedules than many other professionals. The key is for the clergy to give themselves permission to utilize this flexibility in the most effective manner.

Clergy may have to educate their congregations at times concerning this need for re-creation. Some church members may judge negatively whatever the pastor does for relaxation be it running, golf, tennis, fishing, or some other sport. The work ethic of these parishioners is not a balanced perspective, and the clergy must be careful not to acquiesce to these standards. Maintaining balance in life means the clergy and the clergy family can be used by God more effectively in their ministry. The lifestyle of pastors is also a way of modeling. How do pastors help the parish by allowing their own families to fall apart under strain of the pastorate?

Affirmation is another critical area of balance for clergy, clergy couples, and clergy families. Howard Clinebell, a noted pastoral theologian, offered this formula years ago:

$$Growth = Confrontation + Affirmation$$

The world and the church provide more than its fair share of confrontation for clergy families. A shortage of affirmation in their personal, professional, and relational lives is a reality for many members of clergy families. During times of extreme stress and demand, little attention may be given to finding ways of offering affirmation and appreciation for spouse, children, or self. This lack of affirmation can take its toll in contributing to a sense of self-doubt and inadequacy. Without appropriate levels of affirmation from spouse, colleagues, friends, and family, clergy lose their balance of perspective on life and ministry. Jesus understood this need for balance. His frequent trips to the home of

Mary, Martha, and Lazarus was one way of maintaining a balance in his life and ministry.

Connection

The third essential element of care that is critical to clergy families involves the sense of connectedness each person has to oneself, others, and God. Jesus was clear about what he considered most important. "You are to love God first," he said. And then, just as importantly, "You are to love your neighbor as yourself." Jesus acknowledged the importance of a sense of connectedness with God, others, and self as crucial to being God's person in the world.

Communication is the component essential to a sense of connectedness. Although making the time for communication with God, spouse, children, and self is a difficult task, it is necessary if clergy is to be effective in life, family, and ministry. Time spent talking with one's spouse about one's hopes, hurts, or dreams contributes to a sense of connectedness essential to the couple.

Isolation and loneliness are familiar feelings to many clergy and clergy couples. Where do ministers find friends when most of their time is dedicated to ministering to members of the congregation? With what couples do clergy couples form friendships?

More than female clergy, male clergy appear to struggle with the issue of isolation and needed support systems. Lillian Rubin in her work, *Just Friends*, suggests men learn early to be independent, self-reliant, competitive, and on guard. Many men are taught to depend only on themselves. From an early age, boys are taught to compete. Male and female clergy must evaluate their need for friendship and recognize that friendship is an essential resource necessary to being the person God called them to be.

Friendship and the support of friendship provide part of the connectedness basic to life as God created it. Clergy must be intentional in searching out other clergy with whom they can find support and nurture. Clergy support groups may be available in the area or may need to be created to combat the isolation inherent in the position.

As Moses sought to lead the Israelites through the wilderness, he was so overwhelmed with their expectations and needs that he struggled to meet all of the demands being placed on him. He could perhaps be characterized as experiencing "compassion fatigue." In a conversation with his father-in-law, Jethro, Moses discovered the importance of delegation and developing competent leadership.

Moses was fortunate to have the relationship he had with Jethro. Every clergy needs a Jethro—a person with whom they can discuss their concerns, problems, stressors, and perspectives. Every minister needs to have a friend whom they view as a colleague. Many clergy find it difficult to share their feelings with a colleague or friend. They do not develop adequate support systems or structures that provide constructive outlets for the daily stressors encountered in their ministry. According to research, during the past few years 70 percent of clergy surveyed reported that there was no one in their life that they considered a close friend. Intentionality in developing a sense of connectedness is essential for clergy and clergy couples to cope with the demands and respond creatively to the stressors of ministry.

Conclusion

The unique stresses on every clergy family are a reality. The rewards of ministry are rich. Clergy and clergy families who will minister most effectively in this frantic world of the twenty-first century will be the clergy and family who are intentional about following the example of Christ in maintaining an awareness of their needs, developing a balance in their lives and ministry, and remaining connected to God, others, and self. It is important to keep priorities in order and to allow this to be part of the clergy's ministry to the church. Life in the fishbowl can then be a means of witness to others of a Christian life lived humbly and with respect for every family member's needs.

Notes

[1]David and Vera Mace, *What's Happening to Clergy Marriage?* (Nashville: Abingdon Press, 1980) 37.

[2]Associated Press, "Humans Newest Exhibit at Zoo," *Ledger-Enquirer* (Columbus GA) 30 August 1996, 2.

[3]Lloyd Rediger, "Triage for Wounded Clergy," *Christian Ministry*, 26/6 (November/December 1995): 11-12.

Suggested Readings

Covey, S. R., A. R. Merrill, and R. R. Merrill. *The Seven Habits of Highly Effective People*. New York: Simon & Schuster, 1994. Practical perspectives that can be applied to organizing, empowering, and accomplishing ministry.

Mace, David and Vera. *What's Happening to Clergy Marriages?* Nashville: Abingdon Press, 1980. A classic work on clergy marriages by two recognized authorities in the marriage field. Contains an excellent bibliography.

Oswald, R. M.*Clergy Self-Care. Finding a Balance for Effective Ministry*. New York: The Alban Institute, 1991. Helpful to clergy in balancing ministry, family, and constant demands. Includes extensive self-care strategies and offers options for overly-stressed ministers.

Rassieur, C. L. *Stress Management for Ministers: Practical Help for Clergy Who Deny Themselves the Care They Give to Others*. Philadelphia: Westminster Press, 1982. Topics include self-awareness, time, anger, and conflict.

Sanford, J. A. *Ministry Burn-out*. New York: Paulist Press, 1965. Examines circumstances that lead to ministry burn-out. Deals with the problem of failure.

Boundaries: The Hazards of VIPs

Stephen Muse, Ph.D.

"Your rod and your staff—they comfort me."

Over the last decade, clergy sexual abuse has increasingly come to the forefront of public awareness. The Shepherd's "rod and staff" are symbolic of boundaries that comfort the sheep and keep them from straying. This chapter examines relationships between clergy and parishioners by focusing on the boundaries of pastoral vocation, intimacy/isolation, power, and spirituality. Clear awareness of each of these arenas provides a means of orientation in protecting pastoral relationships while allowing the intimacy that is part of all authentic relationships in Christ.

When John was moving into the office of his first parish, located in the parsonage not far from the church, he found a note in the desk addressed "To the next pastor." Holding it in his hands as if he'd found a treasure map, he opened it carefully and began reading.

The author's handwriting was neat and orderly on the unlined white paper. There was information about the 100-year-old rambling Victorian farmhouse: where the water leaked around the stones in the foundation during winter when the snow melted, the age of the hot water heater, and when the kitchen had last been remodeled. Various fruit trees and shrubbery in the yard were identified. It was a thoughtful note from the previous tenant whose kindness made John feel a little more welcomed.

There was a P.S.: "If your car is in the driveway, then you aren't working; and if your car is not in the driveway, then you aren't working. Also, be sure you hang pajamas on the line even if you don't sleep in them." This phrase sort of flapped in the breeze of John's mind as the winds of his imagination took flight to explain his predecessor's advice. A few months later the pastor before the one who left the note in the desk met John and added his caution: "Don't leave your car on the side of the road if you visit widows or divorcees alone."

These instructions came long before the public outcry against clergy for sexual abuse of parishioners began to gain momentum in the late 1980s. Certainly there is a tendency to gossip in the parish, and all ministers know the pain that malicious talk can cause. Much of it is untrue, and most ministers learn how to let it roll off their backs in order to survive in parish ministry. Unfortunately, a small but significant minority of clergy are at fault for taking advantage of the emotional vulnerability of their parish members. Sometimes it is a one-time unintentional slip; often it is not. But in either case, the violation of personal and sexual boundaries between minister and parishioner is accompanied by violations of the boundaries related to vocation, loss of intimacy, abuse of power, and a declining prayer and spiritual life. Because of the important position of trust that clergy have, the authority that is unconsciously projected onto them by parishioners, and its usefulness as a pneumonic device, I call these the "hazards of VIPs": vocation, intimacy, power, and spirituality. Clarity regarding these four cornerstones of protecting boundaries in parish ministry can go a long way toward preventing problems.

Professional Violations: Epidemic Proportions

Conservative estimates are that 10% of professionals, including clergy, physicians, therapists, professors, and attorneys, violate the boundaries of their professional responsibilities every year by having sex with their clients. According to estimates, this behavior involves about 400,000 women a year in the U.S. alone.[1] And because most men are repeaters of this violation, those numbers easily increase to more than 1,000,000.

Consider that in one group of persons sexually violated by clergy (n=25), the collective cost for psychotherapy was in excess of $250,000.[2] Using this figure as an estimate, the cost of getting psychotherapy to deal with the problems of those 1,000,000 women would be somewhere in the neighborhood of 10 billion dollars for psychological services alone.

Litigation is another expense to the community. Estimates are that only about 10% of those women who are sexually abused actually file suit, but as public awareness grows, these numbers increase. In the state of Georgia, for example, from 1990 to 1993, sexual harassment cases filed rose from 186 to more than 400—an increase of 200%. Over a 10-year period the Roman Catholic Church has paid out more than $500,000,000 in settlements for clergy sexual abuse cases.[3]

If those 1,000,000 women decided to sue, the damage to the church and various professional organizations in the U.S. would have a significant economic impact, easily bankrupting organizations. Even if they do not sue, the pain and suffering caused to them and through them to their children, families, and communities is enormous.

Vocation: Set Apart for Ministry

There is no holiness without boundaries. The Sermon on the Mount begins from a place high on a mountain with the disciples "called apart" from the people. The Hebrew word *Qadesh*, which is often translated into English as "holy," means "called apart." Holiness is a boundary. Israel was "set apart" by God as a holy nation. Jesus expected his disciples, who would be living in the new community of the Kingdom of God, to endure the kind of suffering that is necessary to maintain boundaries that set them apart so as to be "in the world but not of it."

Authentic pastoral ministry involves this kind of apartness. Moses, Elijah, Jeremiah, and Jesus all knew this. "Called-apartness" has to do with maintaining one's "response-ability" to be in more intimate communion with others without abusing it in any way. It is a reversal of the "fall" in which we have been called apart from God and others by sin and such intimacy is compromised or destroyed entirely. It is a restoration of the loss of communion. It is an apartness that allows ministers to be on intimate terms of life, yet without taking advantage of or abusing it in any way. Without maintaining clear boundaries in a variety of areas, this is not possible.

The vocation of pastoral ministry has both conscious and unconscious dimensions. Knowing oneself is very important if one is to be intimate without losing awareness of the boundaries that safeguard

111

such intimacy from being destructive. Jesus was intimate with women in ways that scandalized the clergy—who would not even speak to women in public, let alone touch them—as well as with men. He was able to relate this way because his boundaries were impeccable from the standpoint of his inner awareness. Jesus knew himself and obeyed God.

Intimacy without Intrusiveness

The rabbis depicted in the Gospels during the first century would not publicly speak with a woman lest they be ritually defiled. In contrast, Jesus recognized that such defilement was not contracted outwardly, but arose from within one's own heart. When this fact goes unrecognized, it leads to situations in which intimacy with persons who most need it is avoided out of anxiety over possible exposure of this denied material to consciousness. It blocks mercy and empathic understanding. A United Methodist pastor with experience in counseling victims of sexual assault observes how such rigidity can freeze the healing waters of caring from flowing:

> What I am trying to describe here is anxiety, particularly colored by our male acculturation, as a female shares extremely vulnerable and sexuality-related issues with a male. We can become so anxious with our own feelings and issues that we diminish personal touch with the victim in order to protect her from what we are thinking or in order to keep these inappropriate thoughts out of the way. This is not to say that pastoral reserve is wrong. On the contrary, a careful and gentle conversation is crucial. But this male anxiety may strongly influence our interior life with an inevitable effect on our work. Our inner static can be so busy us that we fail in allowing space for the victim. To paraphrase Henri Nouwen, we can practice hospitality or respect for the other only when we can touch our own feelings and so create a listening space for the other.[4]

If male ministers are going to minister effectively to women, the distinction between minister and parishioner that is rooted in the ministerial vocation must remain clear at all times. Ministers function as representatives of the Good Shepherd, and taking care of the sexual and romantic needs of one's parishioners is not part of the call to ministry. To see this clearly, ministers must work to keep the well-springs of ministry free of unconscious distortions.

Violation of vocational boundaries is subtle and happens slowly over time. It involves a confusion of motivations for ministry, loss of self-esteem, isolation, and the crushing weight of the world's pain in a sensitive heart that has lost the distinction between self and God. When ministers lose the distinct "set-apartness" in life that is the basis of the call to ministry, they have lost their "salt." Instead of leavening the world, the world leavens them.

There is a saying among monks that "if you go into the desert without being called by God, you will go mad." Another way of saying that is, "If you lose an authentic sense of intimacy with a community, you will almost certainly develop an addiction." Passions will take root in the place of the heart where the Spirit is supposed to dwell. The Eastern Orthodox Christian tradition defines as evil anything that is not in communion with God. Therefore, any action that does not lead toward communion with God is wrong. Following ethical guidelines and maintaining boundaries require continual awareness of and struggle with passions in a confessional context. The motivation for such struggle is seriously eroded after an authentic sense of pastoral vocation is lost and a growing isolation urges ministers toward using their power and authority to meet their own needs for intimacy in the guise of rescuing parishioners from their pain. This can be particularly difficult in the case of a female parishioner who deeply admires her male minister and is benefiting from what she believes to be his genuine interest in her as a person and not as a means of sexual ministrations to himself.

Isolation and the Dangers of One-Way Intimacy

Isolation has been used for many different reasons. It has been used as a means of deprivation or punishment and to penalize prisoners and brainwash soldiers. On the other hand, isolation has been intentionally sought out by lovers of God, such as monks, as a means of devoting one's whole being to the relationship with God. What is the difference?

Lane Boring had been a pastor for more than thirty years. During that time he had lost his wife, and his kids had grown up and left home and, because of his irascible nature, had in effect cut themselves off from him. He was deeply wounded and equally proud, rarely allowing other clergy to get to know him. At clergy gatherings he flamboyantly played the scholar and debater, which earned him a reputation. One clergyman who had known Lane for a number of years expressed frustration by the emotional imperviousness he had sensed over time. According to this brother, "He doesn't let anyone close. The minute you think you sense an opening and begin to respond, he shuts down or turns to sarcasm. I've never seen him cry, and yet he's always there to listen if anyone else is hurting. I just don't understand him."

Overdosing on one-way intimacy is one of the great dangers of clergy who are isolated. It feels good to be of help to others in need. When our own emotional reserves are low, listening to someone else's pain can provide a kind of relief. When we can be involved in the work of caring, our call as pastors is affirmed, and our self-esteem is restored. Our own problems fade into the background, and we may not recognize the emptiness and loneliness within until it is too late.

Dr. Boring was in a situation familiar to many clergy. At one recent meeting, 70 percent of the clergy surveyed said they did not have a close friend.[5] As it turns out, I was seeing one of Dr. Boring's parishioners in therapy. Some months before, he had been concerned about her depression, which had gone beyond what he felt he was comfortable handling and referred her to me. She had numerous issues dating from childhood that were interfering with her marriage. Working hard to identify these, eventually she risked sharing the pain of her sexual victimization as a young girl, subsequent rape, and promiscuity as an adult. Because of her growing Christian convictions and developing prayer life, she began to feel much peace and hope of a new life. It was at this point that she began to talk about her relationship with Dr. Boring.

Unbelievably, she found he was responding to her increased desire for spiritual growth and mentoring from him as her pastor as an invitation (or opportunity) for a sexual relationship. At first she had been pleased by the special attention he gave her, suggesting books to read and talking with her in his office late at night. It did not occur to her that there was anything unusual about this. Her husband had complained, but felt guilty for criticizing her newfound commitment to Christ. Then suddenly one night, the pastor told her of how lonely he was. He put his arms around her and tried to kiss her, even when she had protested.

Greatly distressed, Martha discussed her confusion at length with me in therapy and how she would handle Dr. Boring. Her husband was furious and felt betrayed, for he had trusted in the man's valuable pastoral guidance from the pulpit. After discussion, he agreed it was important that she set her own boundaries and make confrontations that she decided would benefit her most. Because of her previous sexual abuse as a child and the fear of resisting or reporting her adult abuser at the time, this was especially difficult for her. Still having a tendency to blame herself, she began to wonder what she had done to cause Dr. Boring to act that way. Had she led him on? Fortunately, she had come a long way in beginning to divest herself of inappropriate guilt and build her capacity for identifying her boundaries and protecting them from being violated.

How could a Christian professional with a doctorate in ministry attempt to violate the sexual boundaries of one of his parishioners whom he had already referred for psychotherapy because he recognized how wounded she was? At one level I believe it was an unconscious cry for help. His own life was out of control, but he couldn't voluntarily and intentionally let anyone know this. He was medicating himself through his parishioner's adoration, using his ministry as a means of avoiding increasing feelings of emptiness and loss of meaning. On the surface he seemed to be living out his vocation. He was her mentor, and she was a wounded bird. He had advised and helped her and watched her grow in her spiritual life, and now he was using her to meet his own needs. Psychiatrist Peter Rutter has examined the psychological dimensions of this tendency of male mentors to succumb to temptations to abuse their relationships with women they counsel.[6]

Dr. Boring was out of touch with the motivations for his ministry. The source of his call had been muddied by unconscious motivations. He was isolated from consultation with other colleagues regarding his own work, emotionally starving from lack of peer relationships, and after many years of "living in his theological head" without paying sufficient attention to his own griefs, he had become identified completely with his public role. Unaware of (and uncaring toward) his own needy private self, he was now in the position of being unable to protect his parishioner from his overwhelming pain. When finally crossed the social and professional boundary by attempting to kiss her, he had already violated the other boundaries necessary for authentic ministry without recognizing it.

Peter Steinke, who worked with sixty-five male clergy over a seven-year period who either had affairs or were having them with women in their parishes, noted the sense of omnipotence that was invariably present as the ministers lost touch with reality of their situations. Steinke found that:

> Without exception, the clergy involved in the sexual affairs asserted that they could have terminated the affairs at any time. But none had ended the alliance until discovered or confronted. All portrayed this sense of omnipotence. They underestimated the power of attachment needs and emotional forces; they overestimated their power to disentangle themselves.[7]

Marie Fortune, Director of the Center for Prevention of Sexual and Domestic Violence in Seattle, Washington, identifies other characteristics of clergy sexual abusers that are typically present as in the case of Dr. Boring:[8]

• controlling and/or dominating behavior
• limited self-awareness
• limited or no awareness of boundaries
• no sense of damage caused by their own behavior
• poor judgment
• limited impulse control
• limited understanding of consequences of their actions
• often charismatic, sensitive, talented, inspirational, and possessing effective qualities for ministry
• limited or no awareness of power
• lack of recognition of their own sexual feelings
• confusion of sex with affection

The Real Problem

Since intimacy with others is central to Christian ministry and sexual arousal is a natural human response to intimacy, it is clear that in and of itself human sexuality is not the problem. If it were, there would be a great many more violations than there already are. A 1986 study of psychologists (n=575) by Pope, Keith-Spiegel, and Tabachnick revealed that 95% of the male therapists and 76% of the female therapists at least occasionally become sexually aroused when working intimately with their clients.[9] However, only a small minority of these betray their relationships as a result. Good consultation and peer relationships are effective methods for discussing any sexual feelings or fantasies that may emerge from time to time with one's parishioners, but problems arise when these fantasies and observations are kept secret and/or indulged. Acting on these thoughts, of course, begins first within the heart as Jesus pointed out. When unnoticed and/or denied, fantasies can grow into elephantine action, enormous in their life- and congregation-wrecking potential.

When sexual violations occur, authentic intimacy of an equal peer relationship is usually missing. The sexual relationship is a compensatory response entered into for a variety of reasons,[10] ranging from a one-time slip in a moment of vulnerability[11] to serious progressive, debilitating sexual addictions.[12] Even when a woman, because of her own problems, appears to have been seeking a sexual contact with a male minister, it remains totally the minister's responsibility to identify this intention and protect the woman while steering her toward appropriate recognition of professional limits and/or personal therapy. The minister may recognize and affirm her yearning for intimacy and her capacity to love while reaffirming the pastoral limits of the relationship and his intentions to remain appropriately within them.

Therapists are routinely trained how to recognize and appropriately handle the idealization of clients as well as those rarer cases where the client may be making advances toward the therapist for a variety of reasons, conscious and/or unconscious. Clergy, by and large, have not received similar training in how to become aware of and manage such transferences. It is important not to shame the woman in any way when reaffirming appropriate boundaries. Consultation is an important consideration for ministers who find themselves in this situation (as the nuances of this kind of intervention preclude a full examination of it here).

Fidelity is an act of the whole organism in community, and those most likely to act out inappropriately are those who are most lonely[13] and who work in relative isolation[14] without sufficient support and accountability—regardless of their training and life experience. Significantly, data reveals that clergy counselors most frequently charged with "inappropriate sexual behavior" tend to be those most highly trained who are "burned out, depressed, or spiritually empty."[15] This professional and personal boundary violation is likely related to the sense of "omnipotence" that grows over time, to cover the loss of sense of value and vocation that has been slowly occurring. The violation tends to happen in conjunction with denial, creating an impenetrable wall around the acting-out clergy who, like alcoholics, cannot by their own will and control extricate themselves without confession and help from outside. In other words, the very medicine that ministers believe they are dispensing readily to others, they will not allow themselves to receive. Those who routinely work with clergy in the capacity of mentors—such as denominational leaders and pastoral counselors— should be aware of the need for assertiveness in this relationship due to the special dynamics that are part of clergy vulnerable to problems in this area.[16]

Pastor-Parishioner Power Differences

While the New Testament depicts Jesus' relationships with women as universally empowering, the history of women's relationships with men has often been one of subjugation, whether explicit or implicit. It has been well documented that psychologically, abusive husbands consider their wives as personal property. Until 1874 this kind of attitude was reflected in United States law, which protected a man's right to beat his wife.[17] Until the turn of the century, English law at least limited the size of the stick used to a diameter no bigger than the man's thumb.[18] Moreover, research indicates that prior to entering an abusive relationship, the best predictor variable indicating the possibility of physical violence is the degree of "patriarchal thinking" in the man.[19]

When an individual trusts another, there is always an increased risk of exploitation. This risk goes up exponentially when the power difference between the two persons is unequal, as it is between a "clergy-father" and a female parishioner. This relationship recapitulates both the woman's unconscious childhood circumstances and draws on collective unconscious gender patterns reflective of two thousand years of previous culture in which women's welfare was largely determined by male power and privilege. Men have often been socialized to see women primarily as an erotic experience and are particularly aroused by female vulnerability, which enhances the male's sense of self-esteem. In turn, women have often been socialized to serve male needs even at the expense of denying their own legitimate needs.

Many women and children have grown up fearing men's anger and, consequently, cannot comfortably and assertively challenge a father or clergyman who is violating them in a sexual way. Victims of sexual abuse, whether children or adults, frequently experience psychic numbing and "freeze" during an assault. An incestuous father or impaired clergyman could easily misconstrue this apparent compliance as consent and continue on with further exploitive advances. Because of a desire to please, children will tolerate abuses by their fathers much like counselees will submit to sexual exploitation in an effort to avoid displeasing the minister.[20]

One of the author's clients was in therapy for a situation in which her pastor during their counseling relationship began to prey on her vulnerability and low self-esteem by repeatedly telling her, "I am the only person who loves you for who you really are." Constantly reminding her not to tell anyone, the sexual involvement that had begun with verbal flirting began to escalate during which time he would take the pulpit to inveigh against the "evils of even a single adulterous thought." As she sat in the congregation, she could not understand the contradiction in this and at the time was unable to speak up against him because of her shame and humiliation and because a part of her "needed his affirmations" of her desirableness.

Jesus dealt with idealizations of himself when appropriate in order to empower persons. He affirmed their relationship with God rather than foster a dependency on himself.[21] Presumably this was partially because Jesus was intimately acquainted with the sources of his own motivations, whereas the self-knowledge of his contemporaries in many cases appears to have been little more than an outward façade hiding an assortment of unacknowledged impulses, which Jesus characterized graphically as being like "whitewashed tombstones . . . full of the bones of the dead and of all kinds of filth" (Matt 23:27).

Worship of the Lord comes not from attraction to his personal charm or his need for our attention, but rather from the pure spiritual and human qualities of grace, humility, and joy that draw life into authentic human relationships. Jesus shunned the kinds of personal or sexual attractions that victimize persons who idealize those they have come to depend on and that turn them into objects. Even when approached for a hug, such as by Mary Magdalene in the garden following his resurrection, he acted assertively to deflect it because of its inappropriateness. Clergy must do the same. It is up to the minister to prevent the relationship from becoming inappropriate in any way, regardless of the motivations or actions of the congregation. This is critically important because, in many cases, those most vulnerable to being taken advantage of are least able to protect themselves.

What has been described psychologically from an object-relations perspective as occurring in the abused child's psyche lives on in many women who were abused as children, further undergirding the sense of helplessness women feel when confronted by a similar situation as adults in relation to their male ministers. In order to protect him/herself from psychological damage, according to St. Clair,

> A child becomes "bad" by defensively taking on the badness that appears to reside in the parent. The child seeks to make the (caretakers) in his or her environment good by purging them of their badness by taking them on and making them part of his or her own psychological structure.[22]

For similar unconscious reasons, when women are in an abusive situation, they may feel unable to confront their abuser. So the context is ripe for breaking the trust and then concealing the violation. Unless the problem is addressed, there is a second betrayal of trust on the part of the community similar to when the child's other parent knows about the abuse and denies it or does not intervene to stop it from continuing. Blanchard explains:

Sexual relations with a parishioner is the exploitation of a power imbalance, a betrayal of trust, and is equivalent to abusing a family member. It differs little from incest. Because it cannot be regarded (or dismissed) as a mere lapse in judgment, admonishment, reprimand, censure, or dismissal are not adequate remedies.[23]

Clergy Abusers as Bearers of a Distorted Image

Sexual violations of a parishioner, just as violations of a child by her father, damage a woman's faith by distorting the images through which faith is mediated to her. Abusive clergy who act out sexually with their parishioners function as bearers of a distorted image,[24] damaging the internal object world of their victims further. Just as it is difficult to blame a parent, so it is difficult to blame the minister and through him, God.

The Lord used his power to serve those who had no power. When the church does not challenge existing social structures in which males have frequently exercised power over females in abusive ways, corresponding damage is done to the image of God as an "Almighty Father" whose "maleness" may subsequently be viewed as potentially damaging. Victims begin to have a difficult time finding any comfort in images of God as an all-powerful, all-loving, all-knowing Father who appears to them to sacrifice His own child, thus replicating the very situation that they themselves have already experienced.[25]

The Spiritual Fruits of Morality

For the first three centuries, in part because of persecution by civil authorities, Christian life required a discipline and vigilance that comfortable modern Americans may not fully appreciate. It was only in 313 AD, when Constantine became emperor of the Roman Empire, that Christian life became wedded to a culture of consumption and diversions of ordinary social life. Monastic retreat into the desert appeared to flourish suddenly as persons realized that Christian life without frequent prayer, moral self-discipline, and intentional sacrifice was empty. Noted historian Louis Boyer writes:

The great innovation of the third and fourth centuries was not monasticism, but rather the worldly life of the newly converted masses . . . Christians now become aediles, praetors, and even— though it had little significance any more—flamines of Jupiter . . . Bishops were no longer treated as criminals, but as important dignitaries by the highest authorities, even by pagans like Aurelian . . . Men who had lost an arm or leg or eye in the last persecutions now used what was left of them for the *plaustra* of the *divus Augustus*. And this movement swept through the entire church.[26]

In twentieth-century American culture the situation of the first three centuries continues to be reversed. Ours is definitely a culture of consumption and material comfort that surpasses even the Roman Empire in degree and availability. Christianity and acquisition of the American dream often are represented as synonymous or at least not antithetical. Persons who seek to restrain their appetites or who retreat into the monastery for prayer and worship without distraction are frequently viewed with suspicion. They are regarded as social recluses who must harbor a hatred toward their bodies and natural appetites or whose introversion is so pronounced that seclusion is a necessity for healthy self-esteem. This is how far from understanding authentic Christian discipline we have come in two thousand years.

For this reason, people desperately need their ministers to provide sober and humble leadership in the arena of spiritual formation. They need help from ministers to sort through the mix of modern psychological theories, the impact of sexually explicit advertising and sexual-political agendas, entertainment, and the fallout from the lavish wealth that characterizes the modern milieu similar to that once available exclusively to ancient kings. As in Jesus' day, we cannot serve two masters. Psychiatrist Gerald May points out in his book *Addiction and Grace* that we are either addicts or obedient to God[27]; there is no middle ground.

Jesus warned that where our treasure is, there will our heart be also. This biblical principle may be understood to mean that where the attention goes, the "I" will follow, eventually bringing the body along. Traditional spiritual and contemplative disciplines that underlie fidelity to the gospel in personal and professional relationships are rooted in the right use of attention or, as it is spoken of in ancient Orthodox Christian tradition, of inner spiritual warfare. According to the two-thousand-year-old consistent witness of the Patristic literature, this practice involves a comprehensive inner struggle to obey God not only in deed, but also in thought. Sobriety and guarding the heart[28] are aspects of continual inner prayer and a right orientation to life in the presence of God. It is recognized that the first fall is within. After that, deed follows.

Thus it is only as one consciously and intentionally obeys the commandments of morality with one's body by remaining vigilant to the kinds and qualities of thoughts that occur within, that it is possible to begin to be obedient to the gospel. Cutting off the thoughts within is an effective means of resisting the temptation of acting on a fantasy as naturally happens in sleep when the dreaming stage occurs while voli-tional control of the central nervous system is temporarily shut down. One begins to reap the spiritual fruits of morality by becoming aware of a different source of empowerment. Keeping the boundaries of Christian life and of the ministry comes from humility that calls forth the Holy Spirit. It is prayer that has caught fire in the presence of the minister's growing awareness of how he or she fails to be able to fulfill the commandment of perfect love. When it comes to honoring appro-priate professional boundaries, ministers must be willing to notice and confess even the slightest movement within themselves that might lead in an inappropriate direction. Otherwise, not being aware of what is happening, they can do nothing.

Psychiatrist Peter Rutter offers a contemporary example of how this is experienced with respect to honoring sexual boundaries:

> When a man in power relinquishes his protegee as a potential sexual partner, he also creates a healing moment for himself. In giving her up sexually, he releases both of them from the secret demand that the woman heal him, an underlying psychological reality that permeates so many relationships in which sexual exploitation of the forbidden zone occurs. At the moment a man releases a woman from this heal-ing demand, he begins to glimpse the possibility that he can recover vast inner resources of his own.[29]

Spiritual growth is a function of the grace of God and the effort of human beings in response to that Grace over a lifetime. Attempting to pray without attempting to struggle with personal passions in order to obey the Gospel commandments of love in all arenas is naive, if not blasphemous. Christianity is not a belief system or a warm, fuzzy feeling. It is, according to the book of Acts, an ongoing way to eternal life that requires an integrated response from the whole person: mind, body, heart, and soul. Treating it as anything less than that dilutes it to the point of non-interest. As the abbot of one of the great monasteries on the Holy Mountain of Athos observed, "A God who does not deify man; such a God can have no interest for us, whether He exists or not."[30]

Preventing Boundary Violations

Ministers are more likely to prevent boundary violations in the pastor-parishioner relationship if they are involved in meaningful spiritual, personal, and professional growth experiences. Following are some suggestions:

• *Seek spiritual direction*: Disciplined self-observation and attentiveness to the Holy Spirit has long been recognized as a prerequisite for the spiritual journey.

• *Take advantage of professional consultation and supervision.* Know the limit of your counseling expertise and stay within it. Make appropriate referrals. Have a network of trusted professionals in the domains of pastoral counseling, psychotherapy, psychiatry, and psychology to whom you can refer with confidence.

• *Treat yourself to therapy.* Clergy frequently act toward their parish as they did with their family of origin. Where there were problems, these are frequently carried over into parish work in the form of unrealistic expectations, need for approval, and pressure to succeed.Learn the nuts and bolts of your own woundedness. What are your triggers and blind spots? Self-awareness can make a big difference in your effectiveness in the parish.

- *Observe a Sabbath.* Refresh yourself on a regular basis. Without some measure of contemplative discipline and faithfulness to spending regular time with God in prayer, pastoral ministry quickly becomes emptied of power and at the mercy of automated habits of self and society.

- *Discuss your sexual and/or romantic feelings.* Acknowledge your feelings toward parishioners to a trusted colleague, mentor, or therapist. Suggestions, biological urges, and needs alone are not harmful. Rather, expressed intentions and behavior defile us and injure those around us. Confession and consultation are the best ways to address persisting suggestions that interfere with pastoral duty. Don't let shame or fear stand in the way of being open about what is going on with you.

- *Take part in a support group.* Seek a group where there is trust among the members and a willingness to risk a satisfying depth of intimacy that includes the opportunity for confession, sharing, and supportive learning together.

- *Become educated on ministerial ethics.* Seek continuing education in the area of boundary violations, including the impact of gender, power, and sexuality in the church and workplace. It is difficult for those who have had power and privilege from birth to recognize how this subtly shapes relationships and leaves us blind to certain things that are easily misinterpreted.

Intimacy is not an evil that ministers should fear and avoid by remaining distant from their parishioners. Ministers can embrace the privilege and trust of intimacy with others on behalf of Christ if the following safeguards are in place:

- They are clear about their motivations for the call to ministry.
- Their personal needs for intimacy are being met on a peer level among family and friends.
- They are aware and respectful of the "authority" they represent in the eyes of those who look to them as models and teachers of the gospel.
- They are aware of the unconscious projections made upon them.

With the proper boundaries, clergy and parishioners may journey into the mysterious depth and breadth and height of divine love reaching out through each of us to embrace the cosmos. To be sure, there are no relationships more intimate than the communion of saints who live with the joy of the divine Trinity in their midst. This is love at its purest toward which all ministry ideally aims, indicating perhaps what the church has always proclaimed: that the deepest intimacy is possible among persons—single, married, or celibate—quite apart from superficial romantic and sexual entanglements that may entice along the way.

Notes

[1]P. Rutter, *Sex in the Forbidden Zone: When Men in Power—Therapists, Doctors, Clergy, Teachers, and Others—Betray Women's Trust* (Los Angeles: Jeremy P. Tarcher, 1989) 36.

[2]M. Fortune, plenary talk presented at AAPC National Convention, Louisville KY, 1993.

[3]P. Mullen, "The Fate of Priest Offenders," *National Catholic Register*, LXIX/40 (1993): 10.

[4]M. D. Pellauer, B. Chester, and J. Boyajian, eds., *Sexual Assault and Abuse: A Handbook for Clergy and Religious Professionals* (San Francisco: Harper & Row, 1997) 157-58.

[5]J. S. Muse and E. Chase, "Healing the Wounded Healers: 'Soul' Food for Clergy" *Journal of Psychology and Christianity* 12/2 (1993): 141-50.

[6]Rutter.

[7]P. L. Steinke, "Clergy Affairs," *Journal of Psychology and Christianity* 8/4 (1989): 65.

[8]M. Fortune, *Clergy Misconduct: Sexual Abuse in the Ministerial Relationship* (Seattle WA: The Center for the Prevention of Sexual and Domestic Violence, 1992) 7.

[9]K. S. Pope et. al., "Sexual Attraction to Clients," *American Psychologist*, 41/2 (1986): 147.

[10]J. S. Muse, "Faith, Hope, and the 'Urge to Merge' in Pastoral Ministry: Some Countertransference-Related Distortions of Relationships Between Male Pastors and Their Female Parishioners," *Journal of Pastoral Care* 46/3 (1992): 299-308.

[11]Muse and Chase.

[12]M. Laaser, "Sexual Addiction and Clergy," *Pastoral Psychology* 39/4 (1991): 213-35.

[13]J. Vanier, *Man and Woman He Made Them* (New York: Paulist Press, 1985).

[14]*AAPC Newsletter*, 31/3 (1993):14.

[15]Ibid.

[16]Muse and Chase.

[17]H. I. Kaplan and B. J. Sadock, *Comprehensive Textbook of Psychiatry IV* (Baltimore: Williams and Wilins, 1985) 1092.

[18]L. Walker, *The Battered Woman* (New York: Harper & Row, 1979) 12.

[19]A. Noga, "Battered Wives: Characteristics of Their Courtship Days," *Journal of Interpersonal Violence* 6/2 (1991): 232-39; M. D. Smith, "Patriarchal Ideology and Wife Beating: A Test of a Feminist Hypothesis," *Violence and Victims* 5/4 (1990): 257-73.

[20]G. T. Blanchard, "Sexually Abusive Clergymen: A Conceptual Framework for Intervention and Recovery," *Pastoral Psychology*, 39/4 (1991) 7-45.

[21]Cf. Mark 5:25-34.

[22]M. St. Clair, *Object Relations and Self Psychology: An Introduction* (Monterey CA: Brooks/Cole Pub. Co., 1986) 19.

[23]Blanchard.

[24]S. Muse, "The Distorted Image" in *Clergy Sexual Abuse: Orthodox Christian Perspectives*, J. Chirban, ed. (Boston:Holy Cross Seminary Press, 1996).

[25]A. Imbens and I. Jonker, *Christianity and Incest* (Minneapolis: Fortress Press, 1992).

[26]L. Bouyer, *La vie de Saint Antoine* (France: Editions de Fontenelle: Abbaye de Saint-Wandrille, 1950) 9-11, cited and trans. by John Meyendorff *St. Gregory Palamas and Orthodox Spirituality* (New York: St. Vladimir's Seminary Press, 1974).

[27]G. May, *Addiction and Grace* (San Francisco: Harper, 1988).

[28]Cf. E. Kadloubovsky and G. E. H. Palmer, eds., *Writings from the Philokalia on Prayer of the Heart* (England: Faber & Faber, 1975).

[29]Rutter, 216.

[30]G. Capsanis, *The Eros of Repentance* (Newbury MA: Praxis Institute Press, 1993) xv.

Suggested Readings

Brown and Bohn, eds. *Christianity, Patriarchy, and Abuse: A Feminist Critique.* Cleveland OH: Pilgrim Press, 1989. A comprehensive and challenging examination of the nature of hierarchy and the distribution of power in the history and theology of the Christian church.

Carnes, P. *Out of the Shadows: Understanding Sexual Addiction.* Minneapolis: Compcare, 1983. A comprehensive examination of sexual addiction.

Fortune, Marie. *Is Nothing Sacred? When Sex Invades the Pastoral Relationship.* New York: Harper & Row, 1989. One of the first books written to address the problem. Case history offered along with composite portrait of vulnerable clergy.

Imbens and Jonkers, *Christianity and Incest.* Minneapolis: Fortress Press, 1992. Examines the role of sexual abuse of children in religious homes and the damage that is done to the child's image of God and later relationship with God as an adult.

Katherine, A. *Boundaries: Where You End and I Begin.* New York: Simon & Schuster, 1991. A helpful tool for women whose boundaries were violated as children and who are struggling to clarify and protect them as adults.

Poling, J. N. *The Abuse of Power: A Theological Problem.* Nashville: Abingdon Press, 1991. A call to professional ethics in ministry. Examines the role of power in relationships.

Rutter, P. *Sex in the Forbidden Zone: When Men in Power—Therapists, Doctors, Clergy, Teachers, and Others—Betray Women's Trust.* Los Angeles: Jeremy Tarcher, 1989. Describes the anatomy of males in power who take advantage of women who trust them. Explores the vulnerability of the women as well as the woundedness of the males who unconsciously seek healing through a sexual relationship with women they serve.

Sipe, A. W. *A Secret World: Sexuality and the Search for Celibacy.* New York: Brunner/Mazel, Inc., 1990; and *Sex, Priests, and Power: Anatomy of a Crisis.* New York: Brunner/Mazel, 1995. Indepth portraits of the real difficulties with celibacy facing the Roman Catholic priesthood.

Coping with Radical Evil in the Community of Faith

Edwin Chase, D.Min.

> "You prepare a table before me
> in the presence of my enemies."

Most ministers and well-informed laypersons are not prepared for the outbreak of radical evil in the community of faith. However, decisive research in recent years paints a startling picture of evil in the church. Jesus' admonition to be "gentle as a dove but wise as serpents" is sage advice. This chapter addresses the most common varieties of attacks on pastoral ministry, deliberate as well as unconscious, and what clergy can do to protect the church as well as themselves.

For seven years Pastor John Howard was the beloved and respected minister of a 500-member congregation. In the middle of his eighth year a member of the church told him that several parishioners objected to his leadership style. No specifics were given. Six months later the same member informed Rev. Howard that there were innuendoes that his relationship with one of the female staff had been inappropriate. Again, no specifics were given. One month following those implied accusations, someone sent an anonymous letter to the congregation that vehemently castigated the minister and implied that "important" members would leave the church if he did not resign as pastor. Frantic letters were exchanged between the bishop and the vestries. Overwhelmed with feelings of anger and frustration, Pastor Howard sought reassignment as a college chaplain. Less than one month prior to his reassignment he suffered a mild heart attack. Howard's family, friends, and colleagues insisted that his hospitalization was caused by a broken heart.

When we think of radical evil, our minds race toward scenes of genocide, torture, or some other massive abuse of power where people are wounded or destroyed. The church on the corner with its gleaming steeple does not immediately come to mind. This blind spot is a major part of the problem. Most ministers and well-informed laypersons are not prepared for the outbreak of radical evil in the community of faith. Decisive research in recent years, however, paints a startling picture of evil in the church and the church's insipid response to it.

Unfortunately, Pastor Howard's story of forced exit from his church is far from unique. Statistics indicate that a fourth of all current pastors have been forced out of a church at some point in their career. In each of the cases cited the pastors were either terminated or pressured to resign. Furthermore, a third of all churches that forced their pastor to leave had also forced a previous pastor to leave. Most alarming is the finding that four out of every ten ministers who have been forced out through either termination or resignation did not return to the pastoral ministry.[1]

In the February 1995 meeting of the Association of Battered Clergy in Fayetteville, Georgia, Dr. G. Lloyd Rediger, a pastoral counselor who specializes in clergy leadership issues, recounted the case study of a minister whose reputation was ruined. His career was compromised by one member of his church who had a vendetta against him.[2] The scenario sounded very familiar. It was indeed a variation of the stories I had heard from clergy in two states and more than three denominations. An insidious pattern was obviously unfolding.

The story usually begins with vague complaints by unidentified persons about some weakness or failure of the minister. In one actual case it was something as simple as, "The minister has not visited a particular member of the congregation." This was later proven to be untrue, but the conflict had escalated, and it cost the minister his pulpit along with untold suffering to his family. Frequently, the complaint is not even identified. Rumors, innuendoes, and threats (i.e., that "important" members will leave the church unless the pastor resigns or seeks reassignment) prevail over objective, identifiable facts. A favored ploy, which usually pushes the conflict full tilt, is a letter that vilifies the minister and is sent by one member to the congregation. Caught off guard, ministers are usually not prepared for the level of destructiveness directed against them.

"Repeat Offender" Churches

"Repeat offender" churches are characterized primarily by the number of pastors during their history who have been terminated and/or forced to resign under extreme pressure. Surveys indicate that the majority of ousted pastors (62%) were forced to exit a church that had previously expelled one or more pastors, that 15% of those churches had eliminated two or more pastors, and that 10% of all U. S. churches have forced out three or more pastors.[3] Without question, "repeat offender" churches have submitted themselves to a pattern of subversively and aggressively excising pastors who for nebulous and often inane reasons are perceived as threats to the power structure established within the church. In other words, the chief characteristic of "repeat offender" churches is embedded in the concept: the power of the few. The relational concept of shared power is ominously absent.

Anatomy of the People Involved

The population behind a pastor's coerced expulsion is most often a small faction in the congregation comprised of only about seven to ten people who are driven by the desire for power and control. "Repeat offender" churches function much like alcoholic families except that the drug of choice is the intoxicating need to control. It is certainly not coincidental that the temptations of Jesus in the wilderness were temptations to misuse his power. The abusive use of power to destroy is demonic.

Systems theory can be beneficial in understanding the relational dynamics of "repeat offender" churches. Dr. Edwin Friedman, author of *Generation to Generation*, argues that the symptoms of regressed persons can also be accurately applied to religious communities. Essentially there are four characteristics of a regressed person or group:

• *Reactivity* occurs when angry outbursts are frequent, intense, and almost kneejerk or reflexive in nature. The sequence is to react with anger and then think.

131

- *Blaming* always delegates the problem to someone else. The complaining and criticizing person or group disavows any responsibility or fault for the problem.
- *Herding* exists when the regressed group or individual "herds" followers or gathers alliances together to sabotage the leader or pastor.
- The *quick fix* method of conflict management[4] is the removal of the irritating subject. A 1990 survey by the Southern Baptist Convention revealed that 90% of the laity claimed that the primary method of resolving a conflict was to "fire the pastor."[5] Unfortunately, unless interventions are appropriately applied to the level of conflict, the congregation will repeat the same dysfunctional process.

Even more disconcerting is that targeted ministers may also become regressed, thereby escalating the conflict and eliminating the possibility for effective resolution. Clergy often struggle within a religious system that requires them to meet increased and sometimes unrealistic expectations. They are asked to sacrifice or compromise their convictions in deference to church politics. To maintain a sense of effective leadership in a role that is afforded less and less respect, ministers become insecure, discouraged, and angry. It is certainly feasible that, in their humanity, coerced and threatened pastors will strike back at their accusers in a like manner of reactivity and ferocity. Radical evil has its foothold in the divide-and-conquer strategy. It is as if two demonic camps are at war. When this occurs, explosion is inevitable, and the wreckage is unimaginable.

And what about the denominational hierarchy, the third leg of the relational triangle, within which the minister must function? Graduating from seminaries that still subscribe to methods of teaching and training modeled on the pastor who would be released into the open arms of the small, rural church of yesteryear, ministers often feel inadequately educated as to what to expect when they assume the call to a pastorate.[6] Without the awareness of and skills to handle complex social and organizational needs such as training in conflict management, clergy too often find themselves trying to be the folk hero Pecos Bill riding and taming the hurricane of acrimonious discontent whipping through their churches. Add to this the increased autonomy afforded the local church and the decreased trust in supervisors whom they perceive as indifferent or uncomprehending of what is occurring, and ministers can experience acute isolation and loneliness in their attempts to cope with increasing levels of coercion and antagonism.

Garrisons of the Enemy

Ephesians 6:12 is a graphic reminder not only that all people live in a two-kingdom world, one of evil and the other of God, but also that to lose sight of the transcendent meaning of irrational, pernicious conflict is tantamount to inviting sinister devastation: "For our struggle is not against enemies of blood and flesh, but against the rulers, against the authorities, against the cosmic powers of this present darkness, against the spiritual forces of evil in the heavenly places." Recognizing the strongholds of radical evil in the church can alert clergy and congregations to its ruinous and perverse presence.

Church members who abuse clergy generally fall into these three categories:[7]

• those who are overcome by evil
• those with personality disorders
• those with unresolved issues related to their own histories of having been traumatized and abused

False accusations, deceptions, and defamations of character are the basic tools of those overcome by evil whose intention, conscious or unconscious, is to destroy reputations and careers of clergy. It is certainly no coincidence that the root word for Satan means "the accuser" and that Jesus refers to Satan as "the father of lies." Because ministers tend to be idealists who find it difficult to accept the reality of radical evil especially in their own congregations, they are frequently resistant to recognizing it or accepting its presence. Jesus' parable of the wheat and the tares can serve to arouse the level of awareness in the clergy. Dr. Rediger observes: "We are learning that there is a level of conflict that goes far beyond disagreement, audacity, and obscenity. There are vicious, evil persons whose intent is destruction. This is the evil we have forgotten about in the church."[8] Veiled in a lack of awareness, ministers can easily be ambushed by those whose prime intent is to intimidate and destroy.

The second category of people who can abuse and destroy clergy are those with personality disorders. Those who have a borderline personality disorder are highly susceptible to behaving destructively. They view the world as either all good or all bad. As a colleague once described this group, "Those whom they love without limit, they soon hate without reason." People with this disorder show signs of marked instability in all their major relationships (parents, spouse, children) and exhibit frequent angry outbursts.

Alternately, the third group of traumatized or abused church members can target ministers because of their own unresolved internal issues surrounding not having been protected from abuse in their family of origin. Because ministers are often seen as moral authorities in the community, they become viewed through the negative transference of the abused members as those authority figures from their past who stood by and allowed the abuse. Surprisingly, these persons often appear to be pious, well-meaning, upstanding church members or even church officials. Since they do not appear to be evil, they can participate in a local church without any outward evidence of instability and yet still be bent on destruction.

Furthermore, because many ministers come from alcoholic or dysfunctional families, they tend to be codependent. That is, they are addicted to the approval of others. For this reason they are hesitant to take strong, assertive action against their accusers. Their surprise and shock readily transform into a victim mentality that renders them useless to defend themselves, or they fall into a victimizer mentality that compels them to match attack for attack with equal or higher levels of aggression. Neither emotional nor behavioral options possess the potential for appropriate resolution of the conflict. When faced with the radical evil of devouring antagonists within their own congregations, clergy must find the balance between the application of the primal, human responses of "fight or flight."

"Red Flags" of Antagonism

Even though those within the church who willingly or witlessly proliferate radical evil are statistically few in number, their disruptive and destructive efforts create untold damage to not only the clergy, but also to congregations and even communities outside the church. In his book, *Antagonists in the Church*, Kenneth C. Haugk identifies several "red flags" that can sound an alarm to ministers before the more-than-normal conflicts arise. When one or more persons in a congregation carry a fistful of these "red flags of antagonism," the prudent clergy will guard and gird themselves without being defensive. Signs to look for include:[9]

- *Previous track record*—Has the person played the role of antagonist in the current or a previous congregation?
- *Parallel track record*—Has the person played the antagonist in organizations outside the church such as the workplace or in a social club?
- *Nameless others*—Does the person say there are X number of others who feel the same way, but refuses to name them?
- *Predecessor-downer*—Does the person denounce the former pastor and praise you simultaneously?
- *Instant buddy*—Does the person seem overly friendly as soon as you arrive in the new pastorate?
- *Gushing praise*—Does the person lavish you with effusive praise?
- *"I Gotcha"*— How often does the person seem to question you in an attempt to find you in error?
- *Extraordinary likability*—Is the person disarmingly charming?
- *Church hopper*—How many times has the person changed churches because of dissatisfaction with the church staff?
- *Liar*—How often does the person fail to tell the truth even about inconsequential things?
- *Aggressive means*—How often do you hear the person use vicious language to impeach the character of another?
- *Flashing $$$*—Does the person conspicuously make spectacular financial contributions?
- *Note taker*—Does the person jot down what is said even at inappropriate times such as during casual coffee talk?
- *Portfolio*—Does the person carry an impressively stuffed portfolio as an intimidating tool of the evidence gathered?
- *Kentron*—Does the person use sharp cutting language and sarcasm disguised as a joke?

- *Different drummer*—How conspicuously does the person resist established policies?
- *Pest*—Is the person an incessant caller, an insatiable questioner, or a persistent suggester?
- *Cause*—How far is this person willing to go to promote his/her cause?
- *School of hard knocks*—Does the person brag about being self-made or having had to fight his/her way up?
- *Situational loser*—Does losing his/her side in an argument precipitate outwardly antagonistic behavior?[9]

Once an antagonist has been identified, a prepared manner of responsiveness can help keep the conflict at the most minimal level possible. Rules of response as outlined by Haugk include:[10]

- Act professionally.
- Keep your distance.
- Be accurate in conveying information.
- Avoid excessive positive reinforcement of the antagonist even for a deed well done.
- Discourage nominating an antagonist to a leadership position.
- Be patient.
- Bridle your tongue.
- Do not recommend counseling for the antagonist.

Although these guidelines for responding may create inner conflict for ministers who expect themselves to love the enemy without limit, it is especially imperative for targeted pastors to imitate the "tough love" of Jesus as he dealt with the Pharisees and Sadducees. Furthermore, while impulsive judgments about any individual need to be avoided, it is necessary for ministers to practice discernment. Arming oneself with the knowledge and wisdom to recognize the silhouettes of demonic forces at work can reduce or perhaps even prevent much of the pain and suffering associated with the promulgation of radical evil in the church.

The Bounty of God's Banquet Table

In determining what ministers can do when faced with either the possibility or present reality of the presence of radical evil in their churches, there are two basic formats from which to choose: prevention or intervention.

Prevention includes first and foremost a proactive approach. Clergy need to be enlightened as to the reality of evil within the church and be well read in the theology of evil. With that heightened awareness, ministers can then empower their local church liaison group such as the Session, Vestry, Board of Deacons, or Staff-Parish Committee so that these church officials will be able to make a stand should a false accusation be raised against the pastor. When an accusation is brought against those in ministry, everything needs to be meticulously documented with all of the information brought into the open as soon as possible. Evil thrives in secrecy, and for the clergy to collude with accusers in keeping indictments hidden under the guise of a "low profile" only exacerbates potential harm. If the church of the minister who is being impeached does not have a policy of due process, the minister needs to seek changes in policy that will guarantee the church staff protection and complaint handling in a decent and orderly fashion.[11]

While prevention is always the best policy, conflict may have escalated to the point where nothing short of direct intervention would even be effective. The chart on page 138, extrapolated from marital therapy and conflict management theories, presents the four levels of conflict within a church setting and the prognoses for resolution.[12]

The "marriage" between pastors and their congregations lends itself well to viewing conflict deescalation, management, and intervention in terms of marital therapy models of evaluation and treatment. While specific issues and incidents certainly play a role in the existence of any conflict, the factors of duration and intensity must be carefully scrutinized.[13] The severity of the malignancy of evil within the church must be determined first.

Levels of Church Conflict

	I	II	III	IV
Focus of Attention	amicable resolution of differences	personalities involved	win/lose	destruction of adversary
Communication	open	guarded	closed	distorted
Type of Solution Sought	consensus	compromise	all or nothing	scapegoating
Level of Anxiety	low	moderate	high	unbearable, often with physical symptoms
Level of Emotional Reactivity	calm	moderate	high, with some turbulence	very high, with frequent hostile angry outbursts
Type of Communication	person to person	person to person and third party	rumor/innuendo	negative letters to congregation, contact with judiciary, gossip, insinuation
Possibility of Resolution	good/excellent	fair	poor	rare without outside intervention

Within a church, those involved in the throes of conflict can be classified into four groups:

• Persons demonstrate a minimal degree of conflict and respond favorably to education about how ministers and congregations work and do not work. They are able to ingest and apply information to effect positive change in the relationship.

• Persons have been in active conflict for less than six months. However, there does exist a significant degree of projection and loss of self-focus that precipitates blaming and disavowing one's own responsibilities for the continuing conflict. The intensity can be substantially reduced with directive intervention of a mediating party who guides the individuals back into appropriate focus. Decreased intensity can lead to a transition into the first group status.

• Instantaneous reactivity is the "norm" for persons in conflict in this group. The conflict has been ensuing for more than six months, and the intensity has taken a steady rise. Emotion without thinking prevents the conflicting persons from obtaining or maintaining self-focus. Even if direct intervention deescalates the intensity, the conflict will likely be recycled within six to eight months.

• Adversaries are at war, and dissolution of the relationship appears inevitable. One or more parties have contacted outside authority figures, and "sides" are firmly entrenched. Intervention at this level is more one of "damage control" than of reconciliation.

In addition to examining the group into which the respondents of broiling conflict fall, it is also necessary to account for developmental stressors that impact and influence the conflagration of conflict. Ministers, their parishioners, and the entity of the church body are all components of a multigenerational family system that naturally experiences developmental life cycle changes. These changes, in their most generic description, involve the deletion, substitution, rearrangement, and/or addition of elements that shift the familiar relational dynamic of the church organism's functioning. For example, the stressors of a church building campaign, the loss of significantly involved laity, the renewed spiritual foci, or the implementation of new evangelistic programs all contribute to changing the relational interaction. An accumulation of these stressors can overwhelm the church organism and lead to unconscious resistance to the inevitable changes. Trouble brews, and evil has found its vulnerable spots when the church does not effectively and cognitively grasp that transition time is vital and critical. Those in conflict too often ignore Jesus' request to watch and wait upon the Lord.

When a minister and a church are struggling with the presence of radical evil, it is not a sign that the pastor or the church is bad. It is, however, a neon light reminder to all involved that a brokenness is evident that can either become places of healing and wholeness in the palms of a reconciling God or weapons of acrimony in the claws of demonic hosts.

The Good News

In July 1977, Rev. H. received a letter from his denomination's supervisor informing him of a long-established church that had experienced such distress and decline due to the rigid, closed-mindedness of its long-term governing laity that it was being given one last chance to transform into a viable, productive, spiritual institution. If not, it was going to be closed permanently. Located in a developing resort area of South Carolina, the church possessed incredible opportunities for growth and revival if the supervisory clergy could place the right minister there. It would have to be someone who could deal effectively with the church's history of constrictive, oppressive, and pervasive conflict within the church body and between lay leaders and pastors. Seeking Rev. H. with his talents and spiritual gifts to become pastor was the denomination's final attempt to save the dying church. With approximately nine years until retirement, Rev. H. accepted the call and the challenge.

Having studied the known dynamics of the church before assuming the responsibility of pastor, Rev. H. was aware of the ruling church body's attempts to discourage new members to withhold financial support from obligatory programs such as apportionments and missions, to castigate and confront former pastors for even perceived minor infractions, and to falsify records of attendance and membership. Armed with a thick skin and a conviction of God's call on his experience and abilities, Rev. H. was surprised when he was greeted quite warmly upon his arrival. Warmth soon turned to ice, however, as the new pastor began modifying church "traditions" by revising the board of deacons to include women. He developed a policy of rotation, by conducting visitations that were bringing many new and prospective members into the church. In addition, he hired a director for the choir and established an exciting, well-attended youth program. A small though powerful faction of "old timers" who had held the keys to their private religious kingdom for decades was literally incensed.

As the first three years of Rev. H.'s tenure progressed, church board meetings became increasingly conflictual. Disgruntled lay leaders sought alliances for their positions against the pastor both within and without the church, and rumors rather than facts about the church spread throughout the community like brush fire. Despite the nearly constant battles, signs of health in the church were strong. Church membership was increasing, some degree of financial stability was emerging, and area growth was continuing to bring the needs and provisions for ministry to the community into focus. In addition, the pastor was receiving support from an equal contingent of members who desired for their church to function as the bride of Christ. Even so, by the end of the third year, a massive impasse occurred, and the church was in danger of splitting or folding.

Caught between warring factions in the church, nearly burned out by the stress and twenty-four-hour-a-day demands on his life, and discouraged at what appeared to be degeneration after all his efforts, Rev. H. physically collapsed and was ordered by his physician to take at least five weeks off. Notifying his denominational supervisors of the situation, Rev. H. was relieved to have both their emotional support and their willingness to provide interim pastors for the church during his required absence. No doubt, the pastor's adversaries were sure they had succeeded in their goal to oust him.

Mere days after his return to the church, Rev. H. was invited to lunch by a younger pastor in the area who revealed to him that his adversaries in the church had brought a whole new set of unexpected and serious charges against the minister. "I sure hate to tell you this," the young pastor nervously stated, "but you are going to have to leave permanently."

"Would you mind telling me why I'm going to leave?" Rev. H. questioned.

"Word has come to me through members of my church that you are having an affair with a lady in your congregation."

Laughing at the absurdity of the accusation, Rev. H. replied, "Well, since I'm sixty-one and I'm sure my wife would agree, that's quite a high compliment!"

"This is no joking matter, " the young pastor continued. "You are going to have to go. You can't win this one."

"Son," Rev. H. responded, "let me tell you something. You're young. You're new. I'm going to show you how to win. You just keep your eye on me. In the first place, I am not guilty. In the second place, they know that. In the third place, they've concocted this thing, spread it, and now I'm going to get them with it. They just laid themselves wide open, and I'm going to get every one of them and this congregation to turn around or get out of God's house!"

Determined to take the offensive rather than the defensive, Rev. H. informed all superiors and church board members of the latest scathing indictment of his morals and ethics. He then requested an intensive investigation of the charges by a committee recognized for its neutrality and thoroughness. In less than two weeks the investigating committee found not only in favor of the minister, but also uncovered the culprits and the schemes they had devised over the years to discredit the current and former pastors.

With sworn testimonies, signed documentation, and complete exoneration in hand, Rev. H. could have righteously demanded the removal of the organized saboteurs from the church. Instead, Rev. H. delivered a public admonition to his adversaries: "We are going to go right on serving the world and spreading the gospel through this church. If you can't work with us, just go on and leave. But I invite you to stay and be a part of the team." In imitation of the forgiving Christ, Rev. H. offered much more kindness than he had ever received from those bent on his destruction. Three of the six main acrimonious families stayed.

Over the next two years the church became a model of ministry to both members and the community, increasing in both numbers and outreach to the poor of the area. Unfortunately, in what his physicians described as related to the physical and emotional stress of his challenge to expunge a church of destructive evil, Rev. H. contracted cancer and no longer had the strength to continue his pastoring of the transformed church. With a church body bonded to Jesus and his ideals of discipleship and ministry, however, the church continued to serve God as Rev. H. had envisioned it could. Now, a decade later, Rev. H., who is retired and has recovered from his cancer, devotes himself to enjoying his grandchildren and speaking words of encouragement to clergy who find themselves in the position of having to deal with conflict and antagonists in the church.

The hard-fought success of Rev. H. and others like him who have effectively eradicated churches of radical evil is due in large part to several significant factors. First and foremost, Rev. H. had a firm conviction of God's call on his ministry to the ailing and contaminated church. Without that spiritual foundation, personal discouragement and frustration would have been entirely too overwhelming. Second, immediate recognition and action to modify the administrative infrastructure of the church had to occur. Without necessary changes in the lay governing committees, neither equity nor balanced perspectives would have been possible. Third, deliberate and consistent nurture of the loyal, faithful, and spirit-seeking members and prospective members helped build a solid base from which growth and change could develop. Finally, the minister's attitude of assertion over aggression, offense before defense, and forgiveness instead of revenge created an atmosphere in which the goodness of God could manifest. Firm, fair, graciousness on the part of any ordained clergy saturate a church with both the strength and trustworthiness on which a congregation can depend even during difficult times. In other words, clergy fighting the presence of radical evil in a church need to remember that unequivocal spiritual conviction, cool-headedness, cooperation-building, and trust in Christ can eliminate battlements of demonic forces and establish citadels of divine consecration.

Notes

[1]John LaRue, "Forced Exits: High Risk Churches," *Your Church* 42/3 (May/June 1996): 72.

[2]Lloyd Rediger, "The Abuse of Clergy: Metaphor or Scandal," a lecture presented at the winter meeting of the Association of Battered Clergy, Fayetteville GA, February 1995.

[3]LaRue, 73.

[4]Edwin Friedman, "A Loss of Nerve in the Ageof the Quick Fix," a lecture given at the fall meeting of the southeastern region of the American Association of Pastoral Counselors, Hendersonville NC, 1995.

[5]Norris Smith, "A Survey of Southern Baptist Churches," Sunday School Board of the Southern Baptist Convention (Nashville TN: 1990).

[6]Edwin Chase, "Clergy Under Siege," *The Bridge* (Spring 1995): 1-2.

[7]Ibid.

[8]Lloyd Rediger, "Managing the Clergy-Killer Phenomenon," *The Clergy Journal* (March 1994): 9-11.

[9]Kenneth Haugk, *Antagonists in the Church* (Minneapolis: Augsburg Press, 1988) 69-79.

[10]Ibid.

[11]Rediger, 11.

[12]Edwin Chase, "Levels of Church Conflict," a lecture presented at the Columbus District meeting of the United Methodist Church, Columbus GA, December 1995. Phillip Guerin, Jr., et. al., *The Evaluation and Treatment of Marital Conflict* (Basic Books, 1987) 146.

[13]Guerin, et al., 6-7.

Suggested Readings

Haugh, Kenneth. *Antagonists in the Church*. Minneapolis: Augsburg Press, 1988. Practical steps to protect ministers from being ambushed unnecessarily by antagonistic members of the congregation.

LaRue, John. "Forced Exits: High-Risk Churches." In *Your Church*. May/June 1996. Highlights the reality of repeat-offender churches that have forced their pastors to resign.

Ury, William. *Getting Past No: Negotiating with Difficult People*. New York: Bantam Books, 1991. Shows the folly of settling into rigid positions in an attempt to deal with conflict. Argues for conflict resolution centered around discussion of the goals and interests of parties involved.

Relocation Grief

Gloria Armstrong, M.A.

"You anoint my head with oil; my cup overflows."

The process of relocation is an inevitable one in parish ministry. As caregivers seek to meet this challenge with those they serve, clergy are often in the midst of transition, but their own grief is frequently overlooked. With time, ministers and their families may experience increased stress that is an accumulation of multiple relocations. Due to inadequate goodbyes, clergy will be less effective in helping others with their own. This chapter addresses the losses and challenges of relocation that can become a means of deepening the effectiveness of ministers and protecting their well-being.

"The sheep are on the high meadows; there are clear running springs; the forage is fresh and tender; there is intimate close contact with the shepherd. Suddenly, there is a fly in the ointment."[1] So writes Phillip Keller from firsthand experience as a sheep owner and sheep rancher. In his sensitive and beautifully written book, *A Shepherd Looks at Psalm 23*, Keller interprets each of the verses, which recount the event of a full year in the life of a sheep.

For sheep, "summertime is flytime." Hordes of insects attack the sheep and turn the golden summer months into a time of torture, almost driving the sheep to distraction. For relief from the agonizing annoyance, sheep will deliberately beat their heads against trees, rocks, post, or brush. Some of the sheep become frantic with fear and panic. Some will stomp their feet erratically and race from place to place. Some run so much they drop from sheer exhaustion. Others toss their heads up and down for hours. Some will hide in any bush or woodland that offers shelter. Some may refuse to graze in the open altogether. All this upheaval has devastating effects on the entire flock. Ewes and lambs begin to drop in weight. Ewes will go off milking, and their lambs will stop growing.[2]

Physical and Emotional Relocation

One of the "flytimes" for clergy is the relocation of those they serve and of themselves. A pastor-friend tells of the day he took his nine-year-old son to his new school. With tears in his eyes, Ricky turned to his father and said, "Dad, you're going to have to pray for me that I make this adjustment." This fourth-grade boy, whose family had recently moved to a new church field, already knew what many have experienced, observed, studied, and written about: Relocation involves some significant losses, and we need the help of others, and God, to make the adjustment successfully.

Columnist Ellen Goodman writes, "We are a nation of movers, founded by people on pilgrimage, populated by those who were willfully or forcibly uprooted." She says it is hard for many Americans today to answer the question, "Where are you from?"[3]

Transience is so much a way of life for Americans that we talk about where we "currently" live, work, or go to church.[4] A survey of 1,000 heads of households in 1989 revealed that 40% moved at least once in the previous five years. Nearly 5% had moved four or more times.[5] About 42,000,000 Americans move each year.[6] That means one out of five people, or 20% of the entire population, moves annually. Between 1993 and 1994, 70% of people age 20-29 moved to another residence; 18% of people age 30-44 moved; and 9% of people age 45-64 moved.[7] Many people over age 64 move from their homes into nursing homes or other assisted living facilities.

A large part of the displacement is the result of job changes, many of which are not chosen, but are beyond the person's control. In February 1998, more than 40,000 workers in the United States lost their jobs. Since 1989 about 4,000,000 jobs have been lost, and at least 1,000,000 more will be lost by the year 2000.[8] Many of these will result in relocations not only to another job, but also to another city or state. This means changing schools, houses, and friends and starting all over to build the network of support and familiarity that is necessary for a family's well-being.

In the book, *Good Grief,* published in 1962, Granger E. Westberg describes the grief that arises out of our mobile culture. Even thirty years ago he reported that one out of five people in America move every year.[9] This rate of transience has remained constant. George Barna writes in *The Frog in the Kettle* that while "the Boomer generation is aging and seeking to gain greater stability in life, the turmoil of divorces, the decreasing likelihood of owning a home, and the constant search for a better, more fulfilling career and lifestyle will keep millions of Americans en route to a new home each year."[10]

When I first began writing this chapter in late 1995, I counted myself among the transients, having made five moves to different cities and states (and other moves within the same city) since completing graduate school in 1971. I knew well what Carolyn Janik meant in her book *Positive Moves:* The process of successful relocation is more than packing furniture and finding a new place to live. It means finding a place to call home, a place where we feel we belong.[11] I knew from experience that in the process of relocation, we must cope with the pain of separation from all that is familiar and, at the same time, face the countless demands involved as we find our way in a new environment.

As ministers seeking to meet this challenge with those we serve, it is vital to remember that we are ourselves often in the midst of transition. In the more than two years this chapter lay in a box on the floor while I was unable to pick it up (despite the editor's gentle nudging), I experienced yet another relocation. I suddenly found myself among the 22.8 percent of Protestant clergy in a national survey who say they have been fired or forced to resign.[12] In 1990 the average tenure of a Southern Baptist pastor was 64.6 months.[13] My most recent tenure as a church staff member was seven years.

In these past two years I have also experienced other forms of relocation. I have been devastated by the sudden death of my only brother and have faced that "long goodbye" with my elderly parents. Both are now in nursing homes, and the home where I grew up has been closed. As is the case for many clergy, especially older ones, I no longer have a "family home" to which I can return. I am learning that relocation not only takes place in the physical world, but it also takes place deep within the soul. Like the sheep during "flytime," I have beaten my head against the realities thrust upon me, stomped my feet, raced from place to place, and hidden in the bush.

Change and Loss

Relocation, whether chosen or forced upon us, means change. Change, even if it is chosen and viewed as positive, means loss. Loss means grief. Grief needs to be acknowledged, accepted, and shared. When clergy recognize these factors in ourselves and in those whom we serve, we can more adequately meet the challenge of ministry with persons who are in the process of change. We begin to be sensitive to the impact of change of environment, change of support systems, and change of identity because we have recognized it in our own lives.

Change brings disorientation. Adjustment to geographical disorientation usually comes quicker and easier than adjustment to the changes in our support systems and in our identity. Long distance relocation means our local support systems have to be rebuilt. Although we may still receive support by mail, telephone, e-mail, and other ways, we will not see old friends as often. We never again will interact in the exact same relationship as we did before the move. The loss is even greater if we move from nearby family.

Moves of more than fifty miles usually mean some loss of community status as well. This can be accompanied by loss of self-esteem and self-identity, which are easily overlooked, appearing as a kind of nebulous discontent or blue mood. This is true for clergy children, especially teenagers for whom peer acceptance and group membership are so important. It is compounded for the families of clergy who have been terminated and perhaps forced into a different vocation. Sunday mornings may be the most painful time of all. There is a lingering sense of failure that must not be merely covered over, but rather worked through until a renewed sense of purpose emerges. For persons called to the ministry, not being able to do ministry becomes a wound that does not heal. It may appear on the surface that all is well, but sooner or later this change in the direction and intent of the heart must be acknowledged in the presence of God. It is not only part of the healing process, but also part of renewal of purpose.

Unemployed spouses also feel the loss of identity since they must rebuild connections in many cases entirely through self-motivated efforts. A career can serve as a buffer to the loss of self-esteem and allow identity to be gradually established in the new environment.[14] However, if the move carries with it a lowering of vocational expectations, the person may be at risk for what Karl Olsson describes as "transitional trauma."[15]

About 51% of all transferees have spouses who work. More frequently now than ever before, as women enter the ministry, it is the husband who is the "trailing spouse." In 1996, 52,700 women were transferred by their employers. Women comprised 17% of all corporate transfers. Even when the husband agrees to "trail," he sometimes does so reluctantly and often does not want to discuss his so-called "secondary position."[16]

Loss and Grief

Once we know there will be change, we begin to react to the threat of loss. We may plunge into the busyness that a move involves; or we may respond with denial, putting off doing even the most necessary things. The day of actual separation can be painful, but it is usually followed by excitement and enthusiasm over new opportunities. It is easy for the pastor to plunge into the work of the church, ignoring his or her family's needs in the process.

Within a few weeks feelings of disillusionment may appear. It is important to recognize multiple factors that must be addressed with sensitivity. Especially close ties with family in the current community make relocation difficult. There are other complicating factors: a parent or older family member who will not be moving, but who needs assistance; a spouse with a well-established career; children in high school; family members with an illness or disability requiring specialized care; and a particularly strong commitment to a religious, community, or social group.[17]

Unrealistic expectations about the move (ex: The move will help a troubled marriage. The new job will not have the same problems, etc.) increase disillusionment. Even if the move brought an increase in salary, the expense of the move may keep any expected benefit from being felt for a year or more. The strain on family relationships can be great. A 1987 survey by Runzheimer International found that 71% of employee relocations fail because of the family's inability to adjust to the new location. The difficulty in adjusting may result in overeating, increased use of tobacco or alcohol, anxiety attacks, and excessive shopping.[18]

The impact on children and teenagers is often overlooked. According to the U.S. Bureau of the Census, each year more than 9,000,000 children age 1-14 and 2,000,000 teenagers age 15-19 pack up their belongings and unpack them again in a different home. Children need roots to anchor and support them emotionally. They need to know they have an unwavering foundation in the midst of change. Moving is difficult for children because it involves the loss of friends, school, and the familiar things that are part of their everyday lives. An article in *Parents* magazine states:

> Toddlers will mourn the loss of their room and of the house they've always lived in. School-age children will mourn the loss of their friends and the loss of their school. Teenagers, along with mourning all of the above, are likely to feel anger at their parents for a major life change that is beyond their control.

How the parents "hear" this and offer support can mean the difference between a successful transplant and one that is rejected. The special pressures of the clergy family "living in the fishbowl" make it even more important to do this. For teenagers, it is important to recognize that a move comes at a time when they are trying to establish their independence. They are at an age when friends are vitally important.

In addition to the emotional adjustment of moving, children have to deal with two other types of adjustments—social and academic. Transferring from one school to another can seem overwhelming to children. According to Susan Miller,

> It not only tests their academic skills, but also forces them to reevaluate who they are and where they fit in. The changes in their lives and relationships can lead to feelings of isolation and failure, or to feelings of greater competency and higher selfesteem. Most will tell you that the social changes are more frightening, more difficult, and more important.[19]

Six months to two years in the new location may be needed to dispel all the negative emotions involved.[20] Without someone with whom to share the grief, "transplants" can get stuck in this period of disillusionment. Sharing feelings of homesickness, disappointment, and frustration with new coworkers and neighbors is difficult, and especially so for clergy who come to serve others. An objective listener, such as a pastoral counselor or a support group can be helpful at this point.

In time, most persons adjust to changes. The place where they are living begins to feel like home. Ironically, during this period of adjustment, the effects of extended grief are sometimes experienced as physical illness. Studies have linked the brain to the immune system, suggesting that state of mind can affect the cellular structure of the body. "It is almost as if the body were turned inside out and the cells themselves were experiencing grief, or fear, or hope."[21]

"Good" Grief

Keller tells us that only the strictest attention to the behavior of the sheep by the shepherd can ease the difficulties of "flytime." At the very first sign of flies among the flock the shepherd will apply oil to the sheep's heads. Once the oil has been applied, there is an immediate change in behavior. Gone are the aggravation, frenzy, irritability, and restlessness. The sheep start to feed quietly again, then soon lie down in peaceful contentment.[22]

What Granger Westberg calls "good grief" can be the oil that is needed for those in the process of relocation. He encourages us to "grieve not as those who have no hope, but please, when you have something worth grieving about, go ahead and grieve."[23] Westberg refers to the studies of Erich Lindemann who described the grief process in the *American Journal of Psychiatry* in 1944. These findings are as accurate today as they were half a century ago. Lindemann's studies encouraged the clergy to deal more objectively with grief reactions in their parishioners. "Those individuals who were able to maintain some kind of relationship with God through regular worship and through fellowship with people who really cared, came to see the struggle as a growth experience which actually deepened their faith."[24]

Westberg notes that persons who are spiritually more mature seem to be able to wrestle more effectively with grief because they are helped by the conviction that God is with them. Some individuals develop a deeper faith in God as a result of grief experiences.[25] Through the eyes of faith, the Lord's words to Abram can become words of assurance to those who are relocating: "Go from your country and your kindred and your father's house to the land that I will show you" (Gen 12:1).

In their book titled *Growing Through Grief: Personal Healing*, Howard Clinebell and Martha Hickman tell us there are five essential tasks of grief work:

• Accept the reality of your loss.
• Experience and talk about the painful feelings caused by your loss until healing takes place.
• Put your life back together by making decisions and taking actions that are constructive and that make allowance for whatever you have lost.
• Put the loss into a wider context of meaning and faith.
• Reach out for mutual help to others who have suffered losses.

Infections of the Grief Wound

Sheep also have to deal with "scabtime," an irritating and highly contagious disease for which oil is the only effective antidote. The sheep's heads have to be plunged under the dip. This is a tremendous task that entails special attention to the head.[26] Once the sheep have been anointed with oil, they have respite from flies and insects and scab. But at the same time, unexpected blizzards can blow up or sleet storms suddenly shroud the hills. The flock and their owner can pass through appalling suffering together.[27] Similarly, those who grieve often have "scabtime."

Clinebell and Hickman write about "infections of the grief wound." They say that grief is a wound to the spirit that affects the body, mind, and emotions. If strong feelings surrounding the grief—particularly feelings of guilt, anger, and fear—are not expressed and resolved, the wound becomes infected and does not heal. Some symptoms of infected grief wounds are:

- severe and continuing depression or loss of interest in things formerly enjoyed
- chronic guilt, anger, or fear
- the absence of appropriate grief feelings
- continuing denial of the loss
- withdrawal from other people
- noticeable personality changes
- psychosomatic problems
- escaping too much into alcohol or tranquilizers or work
- a feeling of inner deadness (probably the most common symptom of an infected grief wound)

To heal infected grief wounds, feelings must be expressed again and again until they are drained. Pastors need pastors, and spouses of pastors especially need someone from whom they can seek guidance and support. In other cases, professional counseling may be needed.[28] Unexpected blizzards also confront those in the process of relocation grief: sickness, death, marriage and family problems, financial stress. . . . change upon change.

"My Cup Overflows"

Shepherds carry a bottle of brandy and water. Whenever an ewe or a lamb is chilled from undue exposure to wet, cold weather, a few spoonfuls bring the chilled creature to its feet, full of renewed energy. The shepherd is in the storm with the sheep, alert to all who are in distress.

As followers of the Good Shepherd, we can provide the bottle of brandy and water needed by those chilled and distressed by the process of relocation. George Barna suggests that local churches must retain responsibility for tracking the spiritual well-being of transients who move from the community and help members locate a new church home. Likewise, the church must be deliberate in reaching out to newcomers and assimilating them into the fellowship of faith. Jesus said, ". . . I was a stranger and you welcomed me" (Matt 25:35).

Susan Miller's book, *After the Boxes Are Unpacked*, is filled with suggestions and encouragement for persons who are moving. All of the suggestions involve being available, aware, approachable, and accepting.

The first days in the new location were difficult for Ricky; but two years after asking his father's prayers, he told his father, with a hint of a smile, "I got so tired of them calling my name and having to go up on stage." He was referring to the academic and social honors he received at his sixth-grade graduation. In the two years following the move, he made new friends, became involved in school and church activities, and found a home where he belonged. His cup ran over.

In my case, a long-time pastor-friend provided emotional and spiritual strength through the confusing days surrounding the termination. He offered practical advice along with prayer. Perhaps the kindest thing he did was to call the day after my termination to invite me to his church the following Sunday. He pointed out that this would be the hardest day of all and that it was very important for me to hold my head up and be present for worship. He even called back the following day to tell me he had spoken with a mutual friend, and she would be expecting me to sit with her. He continued to call for several weeks, encouraging me to be present on Sunday morning. How easy it would have been to hide in the bush, but my shepherd-friend poured the oil of interest and support upon my head and offered the water of shared faith, in God and in me, to renew my energy. He gave me advice on finding work and put me in touch with denominational attorneys and advisors who guided me through the severance negotiations. In his prayer he reminded me that my calling is broader than to a specific congregation. In addition, a pastoral counselor walked with me almost weekly for two years on my journey of relocation to a life without a big brother on this earth, without a homeplace to visit, without a "vocational" ministry, and for a time, without a church home. Her kind and gentle spirit, her listening heart, and her "fervent, effectual prayer" were, indeed, an anointing oil.

Today my cup overflows. I have a new position in which I am experiencing God's redeeming grace and mercy as my healing continues. I have survived the painful days of relocation with my physical, emotional, and spiritual strength intact. I have felt God's presence with me through it all, and I am learning the truth of Oswald Chambers' admonition:

It is no use to pray for the old days; stand square where you are and make the present better than any past has been. Base all on your relationship to God and go forward, and presently you will find that what is emerging is infinitely better than the past ever was.[29]

A woman named Eleanor expressed eloquently the needs of those who grieve. Her words provide counsel for clergy who minister to those in the process of relocation and remind caregivers of their own needs.

In the crisis of life, when sadness has its way with us, when our hearts are heavy and long thoughts of loneliness claim us, we welcome the trusted friend or the sympathetic stranger who walks, or sits, or waits with us.

When I suffer grief because of loved ones gone to death or distance, come with quiet spirit for I am sad; I feel the quick sharp thrusts of hurt; in time my loneliness will mellow. Walk with me, but do not hurl your trite words against my weakened soul. Loss through separation for whatever cause is death to me; death to my spirit and my soul; death to companionship and close arms in love.

When I am angry, let me vent my hate, to free my burdened feelings from the barbs that penetrate my soul, my heart, my hope, and joy. When I am lonely and feel sorry for myself, when the devils of my lesser self arise, do not rebuke, but wait patiently, and do not think me only coward; a stronger self will soon arise, the heated moments soon will pass, and pass more quickly then by far, because you wait and trust and listen through the gloom. You hope, you smile, you nod; you suffer, too, with me. Surely then your waiting and your patience is of God; no mortal being can know these things alone, no mortal touch alone can heal.

Notes

[1]Phillip Keller, *A Shepherd Looks at Psalm 23* (Grand Rapids: Zondervan, 1970) 114.

[2]Ibid., 115–16.

[3]Ellen Goodman, "Nomads Gather for the Feast," *Ledger-Enquirer* (Columbus GA) 25 November 1997, A-11.

[4]Baptist Press, "Constant Change Thwarts Long-Term Commitment," *The Alabama Baptist* (Birmingham AL) January 1996, 13.

[5]Web Bryant, "USA Snapshots," *USA Today* (Arlington VA) May 1989, D-1.

[6]"Post Office to Confirm Change at Old and New Addresses," *Columbus Ledger-Enquirer* (Columbus GA) 25 October 1997.

[7]Haya El Nasser and Paul Overberg, "Looking Ahead: A 'Settling Down' as Boomers Age," *USA Today* (Arlington VA) 8 March 1996, A-6.

[8]*Parade Magazine,* 29 March 1998.

[9]Westberg, Granger E., *Good Grief* (Philadelphia: Fortress Press, 1962) 12-14.

[10]George Barna, *The Frog in the Kettle* (Ventura CA: Regal Books, 1990) 192-93.

[11]Carolyn Janik, *Positive Moves* (New York: Weitenfeld and Nicholson, 1988) xi.

[12]Religious News Service, "Large Percentage of Clergy Fired or Forced to Resign," *The Alabama Baptist* (Birmingham AL) January 1996, 3.

[13]Stephen Cloud, "Longer Tenure for the Pastor Means Growth for the Church," *The Alabama Baptist* (Birmingham AL) 1 January 1996, 9.

[14]Janik, 132-34.

[15]Karl Olsson, *When the Road Bends* (Minneapolis: Augsburg, 1979) 32.

[16]Carol Kleiman, "Job Relocation Can Strain Marriage," *Columbus Ledger-Enquirer* (Columbus GA) 9 February 1998, D-3.

[17]Janik, 161.

[18]Ibid., 139.

[19]Susan Miller, *After the Boxes Are Unpacked,* (Colorado Springs CO: Focus on the Family Publishing, 1995) 114-16.

[20]Janik, 139.

[21]Geoffrey Cowley with Lisa Brown, Judy Howard, and Ellen Blum Barich, "Body and Soul," *Newsweek,* 7 November 1988, 89.

[22]Keller, 116.

[23]Westberg, 64.

[24]Ibid., 18-19.

[25]Ibid., 20.

[26]Keller, 118.

[27]Ibid., 125.

[28]Howard Clinebell and Martha Hickman, *Growing Through Grief: Personal Healing* (Nashville: UMCom Productions).

[29]Quoted in Miller, 148.

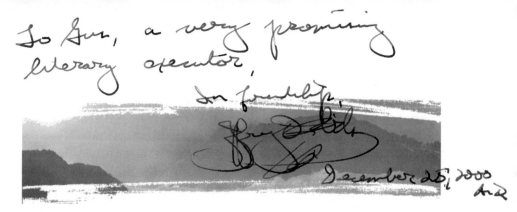

Preaching as Pastoral Care

Jeffrey Wilson, M.Div, M.Litt.

"Surely goodness and mercy shall follow me
all the days of my life, and I shall dwell
in the house of the Lord
my whole life long."

Authentic preaching is born of dwelling in the house of the Good Shepherd, rather than just visiting there, even if for 70-80 hours a week. Proclamation of the gospel with power and authenticity in the marketplace proceeds from living out Psalm 23 with integrity. Ministers must know themselves, spend time in prayer and Scripture, honor the ethical boundaries of ministry, and accept ministry themselves in order to proclaim the Good News cleanly and clearly, not only with what they say, but with who they are. The medium of the minister's own life is the majority of the message.

When I was a college student, I was convicted of the need to grow in my prayer life. I was studying in a city where a distinguished reformed preacher was exercising pastoral ministry. I was moved spiritually when I attended the worship services he led. He was skillful in the pulpit, and his church prayers had even been published. He seemed friendly and accessible, so I asked for an interview. I told him about my conviction and asked him if he could guide me in my prayer life. He told me that he really had no private prayer life. He looked me in the eye, and said, "You might say public prayer is my thing."

On a later occasion I was with this same pastor in company with a small group of other reformed ministers. The subject of prayer came up, and the same distinguished clergyman told us that he did not believe in intercessory prayer, or praying for one another. It was a presumption, he said, to pray for someone else. I stopped attending that minister's church. His preaching was fine. He led worship with dignity and reverence. The hymns came from a tradition that I understood and with which I resonated. Everything looked and sounded fine, but my experience with the minister himself led me to think he was not dwelling in the house of the Lord, rather that he was only visiting there. His visits were both artful and sincere, but they were nevertheless visits and not dwelling.

This fundamental disjunction between what happens on Sunday morning and what happens the rest of the week is endemic among preachers and, not surprisingly, among the American church. If 80% of Americans call themselves Christians, why doesn't our country look Christian? The answer is that we only visit the house of the Lord; we don't dwell there. The difference between dwelling in the house of the Lord and just visiting there is often subtle and difficult to discern. We can spend seventy to eighty hours a week as many ministers do just visiting.

Everyone knows the difference between where we live and where we visit. Most of us have had an experience of hominess in someone else's home, perhaps during adolescence or during a life crisis or after a move to a new region. We say to our hosts, "This is like a second home to me." We mean that we experience a sense of belonging, acceptance, and love of which we are not getting enough in the place where we actually live. In the same way the place we live can become a place of estrangement, a place that has lost its hominess. A parent might say to such an estranged teenager, "I began to wonder if you still lived here." A person who travels a great deal for work may experience a measure of estrangement on every reentry into the place where s/he lives. Home is not merely "where you hang your hat." Home truly is "where the heart is." The question is then, "Are our hearts in the house of the Lord?" If they are, then we are dwelling there. If our hearts are elsewhere, then we only visit the house of the Lord no matter how much time and energy we spend in the Lord's name.

I am a gardener. I enjoy growing tomatoes, and I especially enjoy the satisfaction of growing them from seed. A few years ago my church started what I call the "1 Corinthians 15:36 Project," based on the scripture that reads, "Fool! What you sow does not come to life unless it dies." After our Ash Wednesday service the members go to a plot of land behind the church building and plant tomato seeds together. Over the next several months I enjoy listening to the accounts of my parishioners of how their tomatoes are flourishing. In July they begin to enjoy the bounty that those shriveled seeds planted on Ash Wednesday have produced. St. Paul, and indeed Jesus, told us that the Christian life, life in the resurrection, is like planting seeds that die and are raised up in glory. That is authentic Christian living *and* authentic Christian preaching. The weekly sermon should be the sharing of the best tomatoes.

The problem is that to grow tomatoes you have to start on Ash Wednesday. There has to be planting, dying, resurrection, growth, and nurture before there can be harvest. Ministers know they need tomatoes on Sunday morning, and having missed the opportunities to plant or having failed to cultivate those plants, they arrive at Sunday morning empty-handed. So they go to the store, buy tomatoes, and hang them on a stick. They deliver the promised tomatoes and go home satisfied. After all, they got their tomatoes didn't they? That is why it is so hard to distinguish between authentic preaching and excellent inauthentic preaching. The marketplace mentality is only interested in the end product. "They got what they came for and at a price they could afford. So what's the complaint?"

The situation is substantially worse than that. The tomatoes that were hung on the stick look perfect. The tomatoes grown by gardening ministers, the tomatoes produced on vines grown from seed started last Ash Wednesday in repentance and austerity, may be and probably are imperfect. They have splits, blossom end rot, and white splotches just under the skin. Not only is it difficult to distinguish between the authentic and the inauthentic, but also the marketplace mentality may lead people to prefer the inauthentically and superficially perfect to the authentically imperfect.

Preaching must be true preaching before it can be pastoral, but the work of preachers is to argue for the validity of this authentic but imperfect preaching in a marketplace that is not interested. To make the argument at all there must be cultivated a viable alternative to the entertainment-style preaching that floods the marketplace and for which there is enormous demand. The hallmark of entertainment-style preaching is personality. The audience for such preaching—for even when gathered in a church, the people have long since ceased to be a true congregation—often devolves into a cult of personality.

Popular media preachers and authors become drawing cards on "Christian" luxury cruises. They have become stars. Their endorsements become selling points for programs and the work of others. They have succeeded because they have allowed "preacher" to be redefined by the marketplace rather than by being mouthpieces for the Word in redefining the marketplace. Such star preachers have so reshaped the expectations of American Christians that even backwater congregations expect their pastors to be younger or lesser versions of Robert Schuler. This reshaping is evidenced in the fact that more often than not the people who come to a church building on Sunday morning are an audience and not a congregation. An audience is passive. They come to hear what is being offered. They come as consumers. If the product does not suit their tastes or whims, they go somewhere else. They may be active and even interactive consumers, but increasingly there is little difference between the television talk show and the God-talk show at the place still called "church." When I call on inactive church members, they often tell me, "Reverend, I have my church on television." Even those who leave the comfort of their couches to endure the relative hardship of the (by now) well-cushioned pew want what they could get at home: church by remote control.

A Christian congregation is a group of committed people who gather together as a community of faith in Jesus Christ. One of the key characteristics of a congregation is indiscernible to the naked eye. In Christian worship all members are called to participate actively, even when it seems they are doing nothing. Watching television is passive consumption. Listening to a scripture reading or a sermon requires attentiveness, which transforms the seemingly passive into activity. As the minister leads the people in prayer, the Christian congregation prays with their minister, wherein they are engaged together with God through Christ. The passive consumer in an audience is always expecting a media star. The only star a Christian congregation seeks is the one that leads to Bethlehem.

The tragic irony about the stardom of preachers is that their projected personalities cease to have anything to do with the persons who have become stars. Though in most cases preachers begin by sincerely sharing themselves, the self is a shallow well that soon runs dry. Over time the personality becomes a mask to be put on and taken off as readily as an actor's makeup, and often with far greater effect. The positive alternative to personality is personhood. The discovery of personhood happens in a way that if not literally opposite is, at least, radically different from projection of personality. The discovery of personhood happens in redemption. Flannery O'Connor wrote in a letter that redemption means that "you shall be everything that is beautiful to you which is to say everything except the inconsistency of sin."[1] Redemption takes place first by eliminating that which obscures the true "you" and then by cultivating the true you that is the you having shed the inconsistency of sin. The third, and far more difficult, stage in redemption is the cutting away of much that is good but that, like sin, obscures the true person who is made in the image and likeness of Christ. Even some of what is beautiful must be sacrificed to the realization of redemption in our lives.

In the tomato patch two of the hardest things for me to do are pruning leaves and branches and thinning fruit. This work is emotionally painful because I am cutting away healthy, lovely, luscious-looking foliage. Not only do diseases and pests threaten the crop, but also does the overabundance of plant growth and fruiting. In tomatoes, sunshine becomes sugar: the more sun, the more sugar. Excess leaves block the sun from penetrating to the fruit, and thereby diminish the quality of the crop. Bunches of tomatoes have a similar effect on one another. Where the tomatoes touch is a home for a pest that will ruin both fruits. Fewer tomatoes also grow larger. In order to get a good crop, pruning and thinning are essential to the production of quality fruit.

On the other hand, to survive, the plant needs a fair amount of leaves, and there need to be an abundance of tomatoes—just not an overabundance or an abundance in which the individual tomatoes are getting in one another's way. The work of redemption is like that. Experiences of Ash Wednesday and Lent are of pruning our lives, getting rid of that excess, even an excess of loveliness, which prevents the proper ripening of our personhood in Christ. The sunshine of Christ's holiness needs to shine into the center of our lives.

It is in this third stage that the discovery of personhood is most opposite to the projection of personality. In discovering personhood we must often cut away those characteristics that we would most likely project if we were going the star route of preaching. This means that preachers in conversion from personality to personhood will undergo the spiritual pruning of the qualities that their most ardent hearers appreciate and even demand. As Fr. Alexander Schmemann has put it:

> The condition for true preaching must be precisely the complete self-denial of the preacher, the repudiation of everything that is only (one's) own, even (one's) own gifts and talents. The mystery of church preaching, in contrast to any purely human "gift for speaking," is accomplished, according to the word of the apostle Paul, "not by proclaiming to you . . . in lofty words or wisdom. For I decided to know nothing among you except Jesus Christ and him crucified . . . and my speech and my message were not in plausible words of wisdom, but in demonstration of the Spirit and the power of God" (1 Cor 2:15). Witness to Jesus Christ by the Holy Spirit is the content of the word of God, and this alone constitutes the essence of preaching.[2]

To dwell in the house of the Lord, it may even be essential to become failures as popular preachers projecting personality before we can become successes as redeemed persons authentically preaching the eternal Word of God.

From Personality to Personhood

Years ago a minister friend and his wife visited a worship service where I was preaching. As we ate together afterwards, I asked them what they thought of my sermon. I forget what my friend said, but I shall never forget what his wife told me. She couched her reply in buffered niceties and then said she had found my sermon boring. I had two reactions. Of course, my feelings were hurt. I also remember saying to her, "It was good that my sermon was boring because it meant I kept my personality out of it." I have a big, interesting personality. I had reached a point where I realized that if I were not careful, people would come to church to hear me and not God's Word. I believed what I said then, and I believe it now. That does not, however, keep me from having a twinge of those old hurt feelings. I do not want to be boring anymore than anyone else. I do not like to fail, but I had to fail as a personality preacher before I could preach as a redeemed person. The problem is that I can be a personality preacher every week, but I never completely attain to being a redeemed person. Even to the degree that the Spirit has led me into the holiness of Christ, I keep running back from redemption. God has been good enough, to this date, not to turn me into a pillar of salt.

How does the conversion from personality to personhood take place? How is it that we can also let the light of Christ shine into the center of our lives? One of the oldest and most consistently given answers to this question is: "Return to your heart."[3] "Return" is a word of conversion, turning from the world and from ourselves to God. It is the realization in our lives of God's promise to dwell with us and to be our God. We come out from behind our masks of personality as we participate in the life of God. Human personhood becomes possible through participation in divine personhood. This is the second half of the mystery of Christ. God the Son descended into ordinary time so that, through faith, humanity could ascend with him to the Father in eternal glory. How else are we to arrive at the house of the Lord? This is what the means of grace are about and especially those gifts that God has given the church as means of communion: scripture, prayer, the fellowship and authority of the church, the sacraments or ordinances. These are the signs and signposts along the road who is Jesus Christ and who leads to the house of the Lord.

Preachers in crisis often pray something like this: "Lord, show me the way! Give me a sign." They are hurting. They are lost. They are also like the man who went to Jesus and asked, "Teacher, what good deed must I do to have eternal life?" (Matt 19:16). This man was headed in the right direction. He was asking the right question to the right person. Already the person falls into a very small minority of the spiritually committed. In those characteristics he was like most late twentieth-century American preachers. The first thing Jesus did was to point him to what he already knew. This is the first checkpoint. God has given us guidance and signs aplenty. God has given us disciplines aplenty. When we cry out for help, Jesus makes reference to them. Have I submitted myself to the scriptures, to the discipline of prayer, to the fellowship and authority of the church? Have I laid myself bare when receiving Christ in the Eucharist or Holy Communion?

The rich young ruler said to Jesus, "I have kept all these things from my youth," and then he asked, "What do I lack?" Jesus quickly identified the garbage in his life that was covering up his heart. The man had to choose between his earthly treasure, which Jesus identified as garbage, or heavenly treasure. Jesus told him to get rid of the garbage, and he would find his heart, his heavenly treasure. The man went away sorrowful because his garbage was his treasure, and he wanted to keep it that way.

The end of the story for the rich young man does not have to be the end for the preacher in crisis. The garbage can be identified and thrown away. The leaves that shade out the sun can be pruned. The clusters can be thinned to one tomato per branch. Too much of a good thing is garbage. What things in your life shade out the sun and, therefore, need to be removed?

Until television changed the landscape of preaching, most Protestant preaching leaned heavily either toward reason or emotion. Media preachers—Dr. Norman Vincent Peale led the way—have increasingly leaned on psychology as a third way, which has carried along elements of both the old emphases on intellect and feeling while providing a channel of communication with the world outside the church. They speak a language that non-Christians can hear, understand, and often agree with. None of these three methods—reason, emotion, or psychology—in and of itself embodies the advice of the Heavenly Father—a return to the heart. In fact, based on the way they work themselves out in American religion, they can even prevent a return to the heart. Before setting forth the path of converting the heart, it is important to understand the inadequacy and often the evil of reason, emotion, and psychology when taken as a sole basis for preaching.

A Critique of Pure Reason

I am a Cartesian man. "I think; therefore I am." I want to know things and to live in the knowing. I have all the natural tendencies along with the background for becoming a first-rate gnostic of the intellectual kind. If a thing is logical, then I understand it. If it isn't, I don't. Not only do my gifts lend themselves to this kind of intellectual gnosticism, but also do my incompetencies. My father gave up asking me to help with the field work after I took out a fence-row and then nearly upset the tractor before his very eyes. I have often said, "If I could have done anything practical, my parents would not have spent so much money educating me." I like St. Augustine and St. Thomas Aquinas. Reading Calvin's *Institutes* was a liberating experience for me. I enjoy preaching fine, intellectually sophisticated sermons, and I do it pretty well.

Flannery O'Connor was an early antidote for me. Not even the fussiest intellectual could deny Flannery O'Connor her skill as a writer, her brilliant and incisive style. I was captivated by it. The next thing I noticed was that her message was nonrational, not irrational, rather something that transcends the polarity of rational and irrational. She utilized reason to transcend reason, to prove the limits of reason, and to show that the most important truths lie beyond those limits. This was a discovery for me: there was a way of transcending reason without contradicting it.

I do not know if I realized it as a college student on first reading *The Violent Bear It Away*, but I know it today; I might have become what Rayber was: "a damned, good man." I might have been a good man who was damned because I was trying to limit life to what made sense. Rayber was that type of gnostic, a typically American gnostic. His understanding of life was as limited as the telescope he loved—a narrow scope of knowledge acquired at a distance. Old Tarwater summed up the problem with Rayber and Descartes and me: "He wanted it all in his head. You can't change a child's pants in your head."[4] The most incredible thing about Christianity is not just that "the Word became flesh and lived among us" (John 1:14), but that he also had dirty pants.

Every year at Christmas I upset my parishioners because I refuse to let the second stanza of "Away in a Manger" be sung: "The cattle are lowing, the poor baby wakes, but little Lord Jesus, no crying he makes." "Reverend Wilson, why don't we sing the second verse," someone always asks. "Because he did cry," I tell them. Most of my parishioners would not recognize the name of Descartes, but they have learned well his lessons. They have divided body and spirit as neatly as any philosopher. They want a Jesus who did not cry and who certainly did not have dirty pants. They want a Jesus who told nice stories and who expected us to live moral lives—a Jesus of discreet categories. My parishioners are working-class people, but they are nevertheless infused with Christianity lived in the head, a religion of pure reason.

This religion of pure reason can be expressed as an intellectual elitism or at the grass-roots level as an isolation of believing from all issues of daily living. Either way it is gnosticism and not Christianity. Gnosticism not only disconnects the brain from the heart, but it also disconnects the brain from the hands—the instruments of love. The religion of pure reason distances believers from all the world's woes and especially from their responsibility to do anything about them.

A Critique of Pure Emotion

Though I am by nature and upbringing a Cartesian man, I walked the aisle as a twelve-year-old in the kind of tear-drenched conversion of which traveling evangelists boast over the supper table. The sermonic offerings in the crusade that served as occasion for my adolescent conversion were filled with nineteenth-century hellfire and depictions of a heaven so blissful that, as Mark Twain's Captain Stromfield discovered, no one would want to stay there more than a few days. For me, that conversion was deep and lasting—in sharp contrast to many for whom the same tear-drenched "going forward" had brief effect and often became an embarrassment soon thereafter. In the run of their lives it was the walk down the aisle that seemed to be the lapse.

Over the next decade or two I observed that many people who are most susceptible to the emotionally manipulative sermons of the tent evangelist repeated their experience. They got "saved" as teenagers, but then reverted to their previous ways. They came back to the Lord in early adulthood, but then backslid. From then on, every few years there would be a new burst of emotional religious fervor followed by an inexorable return to their previous vices, usually fleshly. I also observed that those prone to this kind of emotional religion who stayed with the program did so by immersing themselves in a religious environment where they got a weekly and perhaps twice or thrice weekly dose of this kind of emotional experience.

I visited such churches throughout my teen years. Most were Baptist congregations (some of which had very fine pastors), but occasionally I visited a Pentecostal congregation. Even in some of the Pentecostal churches where I found the spiritual diet vulgar and repulsive, I sensed that there was something genuine that I did not have in my own strait-laced Presbyterian tradition. At the same time I perceived that there was something extremely unhealthy in promoting emotional experiences as a norm of Christian worship and devotion. I was extremely fortunate (as always saved by an unlooked-for grace) because my own life had been touched in a healthy way by emotional Christianity. Perhaps it did me good because it was alien to me and contrary to my nature and inclinations. I had no desire to persist in the steady stream of religious emotion that I observed.

In later years I came to understand that for many people, Karl Marx was correct: religion is their opiate. The inducement of certain emotions often affects body chemistry. When people say that they are "high on Jesus," they are often literally correct. The emotions they experience in worship trigger a fix. They grow chemically dependent upon their religion. When religion becomes pure emotion, it has also become pure dope.

A Critique of Pure Psychology

The senior pastor of a 6,000-member mainline church once told me that preaching is "group counseling done *en masse*." The preacher as psychologist has emerged as one of the most popular paradigms in late twentieth-century American Protestantism. Though first embraced by more liberal Christians, the enormous media success of Dr. James Dobson has opened the doors of many conservative churches to the preacher as psychologist. The prevalence of casual psychology and the extent to which psychological terms of art have become cultural buzzwords has made it nearly impossible for preachers most resistant to the psychological method to remain untouched by psychology. Counseling or therapy has become the secular sacrament of confession for countless Protestants.

The United States of America is arguably the most analyzed society in the history of the world, both as individuals and as a nation. If the psychological method is so valuable (a tenet we may assume as a premise in nearly any debate touching upon psychology), then why are our lives such a mess? People often undergo years of psychological therapy without changing their lives. They understand everything, but they are living in the same patterns. Preachers who seek to function as pop-psychologists in the pulpit are generally popular both in run-of-the-mill congregations and in megachurches, in book sales, and in the popularity of their electronic media appearances. Despite the baptism of the psychological method, Christians go on getting divorced, doing business like used car salespeople, defining themselves by what they consume and, in general, living in a state of confusion—or "quiet desperation," as Thoreau put it. Why?

The reason is that psychology has become a substitute for conversion. Analysis without conversion is inadequate and dangerous. The understanding of the dynamics of people's personalities and of their interrelational dynamics with others is a tool of power. Wielding that tool without conversion becomes a force of evil. Scott Peck states as the first sentence of his book, *People of the Lie,* "This is a dangerous book . . . some may use its information to harm others."[5] The psychological method can become a tool for evil in the hands of the unconverted. Their knowledge enables them to become better manipulators of those with whom they relate.[6]

The greatest danger of pure psychology—understanding without conversion—is not "analysis paralysis," but the use of the psychology to gain control over other people. Seeing preaching as group psychology is especially dangerous because the sermon ceases to be authentic preaching and can become an agency for evil. Instead of being a Christian Dr. Freud, the preacher as pop-psychologist runs the risk of becoming an amiable Dr. Goebbels by projecting her own personality onto the congregation. In such cases the preacher becomes, however unwittingly, an example of the Fuehrer principle in action rather than a mouthpiece for the Word of God. The senior pastor who exudes charm in the pulpit and on the golf course with his richest parishioners but who is intolerable in the church office or at home with his family is both victimizer by and the victim of understanding without conversion, of pure psychology.

A Heart Purified by the Word of God

Jesus said, "For where your treasure is, there your heart will be also" (Matt 6:21). The answer lies in the location of one's treasure. Is treasure a full church, a big church, an affirming church, the frequent courting of pastoral search committees, building new facilities, being considered a mover and shaker in one's denomination, getting people to do as they are told, being a star? If so, then that is where one's heart is also. If treasure is the Word of God and the hope of dwelling in the house of the Lord forever, then that is where one's heart is. Every preacher needs to ask: "Where is my heart?"[7]

What is the heart? Laidlaw sums up the biblical view of the heart as "man's entire mental and moral activity, both the rational and the emotional elements . . . the hidden springs of the personal life."[8] The heart embraces both intellect and emotion, the ego and psyche, a person's whole being. The heart is the home of the real humanity of each person. The heart is the source of moral and spiritual life. It is the seat of grief, joy, desires, affections, perceptions, thoughts, understanding, reasoning, imagination, conscience, intentions, purpose, faith, and will.[9] Andre Louf describes the heart as "the inmost core of our being."[10]

Once we have pondered the meaning of the heart, we can understand more truly the word "courage," which is derived from the Latin word for heart. In its most fundamental etymological meaning, courage is an act of the heart, the engagement of the whole person for a purpose greater than oneself. A life led by the heart is, by definition, a courageous life. Cowardice, apathy, and bullying are the alternatives to courage; they are denials of the heart. They are denials of a person's innermost self and fundamental humanity. To be human is to be courageous. To be a preacher of the Word is to be courageous.

It is all too easy for preachers to lose heart. They have, in the same literal and etymological sense, become discouraged and disheartened. They have had the heart taken out of them. At the same time people in our culture have a need greater than ever before to have the heart put back into them, namely, to be encouraged. But instead of being encouraged, they are discouraged more and more. Preaching is pastoral care when it puts the heart back into people. Before preachers can put the heart back into others, they must find their own hearts.

Everyone has a heart, but where is it? All too often the heart is covered up, sometimes at the bottom of a garbage dump. Other times it is covered by the green superabundance of goodness. We may be afraid to find our hearts because we are afraid to live differently than we now do. However much pain we are experiencing, we often prefer to live in "quiet desperation"[11] with a cosmetic façade (personality) that gives the appearance of all being well. When the cosmetic façade is pointed to, when the garbage is talked about, people—preachers included—often become angry. Few of us want to live according to the heart whether we are shepherds or sheep. Resistance to living according to the heart is seated in the treasuring of garbage. If garbage is treasured, we are understandably reluctant to throw it out.

We live in a day of medical miracles, of which a heart transplant is one. Ezekiel received a word from God that discussed a heart transplant—not a physical heart transplant, but a heart transplant of the inner person, the fundamental humanity of a person. "A new heart I will give you, . . . and I will remove from your body the hart of stone and give you a heart of flesh" (36:26). Encouragement, or putting the heart back into someone, is conversion. Conversion has too often been reduced to an intellectual acceptance of the claims of Christianity or to an emotional experience or to an explanation of why I am the way I am. Conversion embraces all three but is also far greater than any one of them. Conversion is an earthquake of the heart after which the landscape of life is never the same again.

St. Paul had that earthquake-of-the-heart type of experience on the road to Damascus. He was struck by the Word of God as if by lightning. He was blinded and would never see the world the same way again. When God gives a new heart, life will never be the same again. There are rituals and events in our lives that often mark that kind of realization: for example, childbirth, marriage, baptism, confirmation, ordination, and the death sentence whether uttered by a judge or a doctor. After the occurrence of these events, the sky is a different shade of blue and the grass a different shade of green. If we say "yes" to the earthquake of the heart, we see the garbage as garbage and begin clearing it away. It was to such a conclusion that St. Paul had arrived when he wrote to the Philippians, "I regard everything as loss because of the surpassing value of knowing Christ Jesus my Lord. For his sake I have suffered the loss of all things, and I regard them as rubbish, in order that I may gain righteousness . . ." (3:8). Paul looked upon everything else in life and said it was all manure when compared to Jesus Christ. Whatever he had counted as valuable before the earthquake of the heart, afterwards he recognized as garbage.

In 1996 my family and I visited Scotland. We stayed for a few days in a Benedictine monastery. Behind that monastery there was a huge ridge. We set out one day to walk to the top of the ridge. My son said he wanted to find out if we could see the ocean from the top; we might well have been able to do so because we were not many miles from the sea. We scaled about three-quarters up that ridge, but got tired and went back down. I have occasionally wondered what we would have seen if we had pushed on and reached the top. We shall probably never know. Even if we should go back there, it may well be different. That part of the ridge had been recently timbered, so we were able to make a pretty quick climb. If we went again, our path might be inhibited by underbrush. The growth of trees might make the view from the top very different than it was in 1996. I was the one who thought we should retreat, but I regret that suggestions now, for I shall never know what we might have seen from the top.

So often we turn back just at the moment we need to push on. We lose heart. We become discouraged when we need to be encouraged. We live in the garbage just at the moment when we need to find our hearts. We need to get rid of whatever is covering up our hearts. It is in the face of such a demand that many turn away extremely sorry because they are rich, not rich in money perhaps, but rich in the treasure of Jesus Christ. Pushing forward is as difficult as it is essential.

The Essential Wound of Shepherds

The Bible speaks of circumcising our hearts. We know what circumcision is. Even for a baby, it is a bloody and painful operation. For the Jew, circumcision is God's mark upon him, a sign that giving one's heart to God costs something. Giving our hearts to God costs us blood, and that requires courage. Circumcision is such a powerful image

171

because it is vividly physical. It tells us that God reaches down and grabs us by the loins where we are most vulnerable. Circumcision tells us that we cannot come to God unless we are willing to be wounded, and wounded in a time and place and manner of God's choosing. Circumcision of the heart helps us to understand that we are talking about the essence of who we are as human beings. It tells us that giving our hearts to God does not protect us from pain and suffering, but rather puts us on the front fine of pain and suffering. Why else would we need courage?

Circumcision of the heart is the wound of self-surrender through which we come to personhood as an alternative to the wound of self-destruction as expressed in pure personality. The precondition for this essential wound is a willingness to have our favorite parts cut off in order to live in our hearts and living in them to be led into the heart of God. When Moses admonished the children of Israel to circumcise the foreskin of their hearts, he told them to fear, love, and serve the Lord and then to give expression of those dynamics by pursuing justice for the powerless: the orphan, the widow, and the stranger. The content of his interpretive admonition is what Jesus called the two great commandments:

> "You shall love the Lord your God with all your heart, with all your soul, and with all your mind." This is the greatest and first commandment. And a second is like it: "You shall love your neighbor as yourself." On these two commandments hang all the law and the prophets. (Matt 22:37-40)

In the similar accounts in Luke's record a lawyer recites the summation of the law and then asks, "Who is my neighbor?" The answer he gives is the parable we call "the Good Samaritan." Jesus follows what Moses interprets as circumcision of the heart: embracing the disenfranchised. To put this another way, in order for preaching to become pastoral care (i.e., being shepherd and not merely a hireling), the preacher must first become a sheep of Matthew 25. True preaching happens only as an outworking of active and committed compassion.

We might have expected the admonition to circumcise our hearts to lead to confession and repentance of sin. Instead, Moses tells the Israelites to perform works of charity to those who can least repay it.

Preachers cannot preach the Word unless they live in their hearts, and they cannot live in their hearts unless they open their hearts to the least brethren. So it was that Jesus on the night before his death held a seminar on preaching and pastoral care. He drove home his message by washing the feet of his disciples.

Finding our hearts and then living in them is the path to dwelling in the house of the Lord forever. Dom Andre Louf writes about the life of the monk and especially the Cistercian monk in his book, *The Cistercian Way*. In reference to the spiritual life of Cistercian monasticism, one could often substitute the word "preacher" every time he uses the word "monk." That is especially true of the following passage:

> There comes a time . . . when the monk will close the commentaries and put aside the dictionaries and concordances. He will no longer ask questions or pose problems. Nor will he run after representations of the word in his imagination, nor lean on the feelings which these can arouse. He will try instead to rest before God in reverent and loving attention, while his interior faculties remain empty. He must work to create this emptiness, this space within, so that the power of God's word can fill it. Only then will this power spring up like a flash of light or as a force which can transform me. This does not normally happen quickly. Perseverance, humility and patience are needed, and not some sort of interior searching and questioning which would be no help at all. What the monk must do is nurture his desire for the word of God in faith and trust. The attitude of the soul and heart which we are here describing is not always easy or comfortable. The reason for this is that it is an attempt to persevere in what is in fact an interior desert.[12]

This is the interior posture of waiting upon the Lord. Dom Andre summarized his thoughts by stating, "The Word awakens the heart." God has given us signposts such as scriptures, prayer, sacraments, fellowship, and authority of the church to guide us along the narrow path. One day these signposts will guide us into a desert where the way is so narrow we cannot find it. Though we are not alone, we are, in another sense, on our own.

Treasure in a Human Vessel

There was an interesting little lady whom God had given to me to help. This was not an exclusive relationship. Miss Atwood lured her way into the lives of many people. She had been physically abused by her father, which was partly the cause of her physical and emotional problems, but also his response to her disabilities. Despite her mental limitations, she often displayed a seering wit and keen insight into the characters of those with whom she interacted. She had a speech impediment, a hunchback, and numerous physical ailments. She was one of the lost souls of the world. I had helped her out of her family situation and then to have some semblance of independence through the various governmental support programs. Numerous people in various churches had also helped her.

I had tried each year to invite her to have a meal with my family between Christmas and New Year's Day. One year I discerned she had nowhere to go for Christmas dinner, as had been usual in the past. After some probing I discovered that she wanted to have Christmas dinner with my family, so I invited her. She was a person for whom one invitation was never enough, so I called about once a week to reconfirm our welcome of her and her willingness to attend the dinner. The Monday before Christmas when I phoned her she was obviously not well, and she said she did not think she would feel well enough to come on Christmas Day. We arranged to talk again later in the week to see if she felt well enough to come. When I got home from church on Wednesday evening, December 23, there was a garbled message on my voice mail. The next day I phoned her and got her answering machine. I left a message for her to return my call. Later in the day I phoned again, leaving a message that was slightly scolding. After all, this was so typical of her, getting people to want to help her and then when it came time, she would go underground until the opportunity was past. Over the next few days I called additional times, feeling rather provoked with her. How could she be so ungrateful?

The next Monday another of her friends called me to say that he was worried about Miss Atwood. He wanted to know if I had heard from her. He resolved to get a sheriff's deputy to force entry into the house. He called me later in the day to say that they had found Miss

Atwood several days dead, lying on the sofa in her living room. I realized that the garbled message I had received were probably her last words in this life. Not only had I been unable to understand them, but I had also disdained them. The next day, much to my surprise, the undertaker called me to say Miss Atwood had a prearranged, prepaid funeral and had stipulated that I was to conduct her service. She had attended other churches in the area, but had explicitly stated that I was to be the only minister involved in her funeral.

Both in learning of her death and then being asked to have charge of her funeral, I was overwhelmed by a series of emotions, shame and embarrassment among them. There were more surprises in store, one of which was how much I missed her. While she lived I had always thought of her as someone I helped, as one of the burdens God had assigned to me. Once she was dead I experienced grief and sorrow at the loss of someone who had been my friend, someone who had been in my corner no matter what, pulling for me in all my endeavors, someone whom no event short of death could shake loose from the fabric of my life. Never again would I pick up the phone to hear her querulous voice asking my opinion about some neighbor or social worker who had gotten under her skin that week. Instead of being relieved of a burden, I was deprived of a faithful friend of whose support I had been oblivious. She had to die for me to discover all that.

Miss Atwood's funeral was held the afternoon of New Year's Eve, the last day of the year. The day was cold, cloudy, and bare-grounded. The undertaker had advised me that there might not be enough people present to carry her coffin. Even in normal circumstances the day of New Year's Eve is not an auspicious time to hold a funeral. Then the cars began to arrive. The two preachers she had said she didn't want to conduct her funeral were there. Several social workers and some of her fellow clients from a mental health clinic came. A woman who had been her schoolmate half a century earlier and a few assorted kin and neighbors also attended the funeral. There were about twenty of us for that graveside service. As the hour struck, it began to snow, just enough to grace the ground.

I read the usual passages of scripture and prayed the usual prayers, but I also recalled her life to those who had become her family and were her friends. I pulled no punches, speaking about the life of abuse she had experienced and about some of the anti-social ways she had responded to life and often to those who were most faithful in trying to help her. The day before I had run into one of her social workers. I had met him only once before in Miss Atwood's company a few years earlier. In the providence of God I met him the second time the day before Miss Atwood's funeral.

He had said how sad he was at her death because during the past year she had gained an aspect of health and wholeness in her life that he had never seen in her during the years he had overseen her case. I reflected on his observation. My initial reaction was to resonate with a sense of tragedy that she had died just when she was beginning to learn to live well. But then I wondered, isn't this the goal of life, to enter into wholeness? If so, then hadn't Miss Atwood died at exactly the right time? Miss Atwood had always possessed a resolute faith in God through Jesus Christ. She had often expressed doubts about mortal man, but never about God. During her final year in this world her faith had become true in her living. Can there be any better time to die? I did not say to the assembled then, but I add an additional word now. Homegrown tomatoes can ripen even on the last day. I had found my heart, and so, I think, had Miss Atwood.

Preaching as Pastoral Care

Since the Lord is my shepherd, the house of the Lord is the Shepherd's house. In the Father's heart are many hearts. Those who dwell in the house of the Lord learn how to be shepherds. Chapter 10 of John's Gospel gives an account of Jesus talking about this school for shepherds. Jesus explicitly identifies himself as "the good shepherd," and thus provides a verbal bridge between himself and Psalm 23. Jesus distinguishes between himself, the good shepherd, and hirelings who also tend sheep but who run away at the first sign of danger. He speaks about his other sheep who are not of this fold but that he intends to bring into the fold so that there may be one fold and one shepherd.

Jesus is speaking both Christologically and ecclesiologically: This is not just about Jesus being the Lord; it is also about the nature of the church when Jesus will no longer be physically present among his disciples. Those who are ordained to pastoral ministry need to ask themselves: Am I a shepherd or a hireling? Both tend sheep and, one could argue, even hirelings serve a purpose. The example Jesus sets, however, is as a shepherd. He condemns the hireling for fleeing precisely in the moment of greatest need. The hireling has a job. The shepherd has a calling. The only way to become a shepherd is to dwell in the house of the shepherd who is both the shepherd of the sheep and the shepherd of shepherds.

Coming to terms with the call to be a shepherd rather than a hireling, the call to dwell in the house of the Good Shepherd and not just to visit there, entails a repudiation of pastoral ministry as a career or as a job. Pastoral ministry is a calling by the Good Shepherd to become one of God's helper-shepherds. It is truly a profession in the meaning that word had until a few decades ago: A minister professes Jesus Christ in the totality of his life. To mount the pulpit without this understanding is an act of shameless audacity, a monstrous fraud. The pastor, or "shepherd," speaks not with her voice but with the voice of the Lord. "The sheep hear his voice. He calls his own sheep by name . . . and the sheep follow him because they know his voice" (John 10:3-4). "The voice of the Lord is powerful" and "full of majesty" (Ps 29:4), but its power is pastoral. The Lord is the Good Shepherd, whose purpose is to bring all the sheep safely into the fold.

The Responsibility of Living in Glory

The word "awesome" has come to be used about the most banal things. Even a pepperoni pizza can be awesome. There are some things that, on the other hand, are truly awe-inspiring and yet are not perceived as such. As preachers step into the pulpit, their calling ought to inspire awe in themselves and in their hearers because they speak with the voice of Jesus Christ. However powerful is the voice of the Lord, this work of preacher-shepherd is dangerous. The danger inheres in the glory of it. First, there is the peril of handling sacred things. The glory of the Lord may strike the preacher blind or even dead. For who can see God and live? Even those who accidentally touched the ark of the covenant were struck down. The glory of the Lord is both wonderful and terrible. The Scriptures speak of the millstone of Matthew 18:6, the eating and drinking damnation of 1 Corinthians 11:29, and the plagues of Revelation 22:18-19. Preachers cannot afford to be careless or to yield to their own unworthiness. The scriptures weave images of dire warning into the proclamation of God's glory from beginning to end.

The second cause of danger is that the glory of the Lord attracts the attention of the world. Whenever the Word enters the world, the world receives him not. The dragon will inevitably come. He may appear as Herod or Annas or Nero, as a member of the inner circle, or as an announced enemy, but come he will. Radical evil appears within and without the church's doors. In a thousand figurative ways and perhaps once in a literal way, the helper-shepherd will have to lay down his life for his sheep. For this, the preacher as pastor needs to return to his heart, for in the heart one finds the courage necessary for "loving the hell out of the world."

Terrible responsibility is incumbent upon the shepherd-preacher: the responsibility to dwell in the house of the Lord. For that reason preachers must return to their hearts, yielding themselves to the pruning and thinning of the Holy Ghost. That is not the comfort most preachers are looking for, but it is nonetheless one of the primary methods of the Spirit's comforting advocacy. Reliance on pure reason or pure emotion or pure psychology have to be lopped off so that preachers can learn absolute dependence upon God. This conversion (the turn towards God) begins and continues as preachers return to the heart, which is God. Because Christ the Good Shepherd is also the holy image and likeness of God, the redemptive power of Christ conveys the glory of God to believers. As believers return to their hearts, they find Christ, risen in glory. Christ in the heart shines the divine glory into the world, and thus conquers the world. This is the beginning of goodness and mercy that are without end. The work of redemption having begun in the heart makes its way to the preacher's mouth. Preaching has become pastoral care because then the preacher can beckon the sheep into the fold of Christ so that they too may "dwell in the house of the Lord forever."

Notes

[1] Flannery O'Connor, *The Habit of Being* (New York: Farrar, Straus and Giroux, 1979).

[2] A. Schmemann, *The Eucharist: Sacrament of the Kingdom* (Crestwood NY: St. Vladimir's Seminary Press, 1988) 78.

[3] Andre Louf, *The Cistercian Way* (Kalamazoo MI: Cistercian Publications, 1989) 71.

[4] Flannery O'Connor, *The Violent Bear It Away* (New York: Farrar, Straus and Giroux, 1960) 75.

[5] M. Scott Peck, *People of the Lie* (New York: Simon & Schuster, 1983) 9.

[6] Peck identifies various dangers of his "psychology of evil" and at the same time points to dangers of psychology in general. First, there is danger inherent in the scientific method because the state of science changes (p. 257). Second, there is the abuse of the psychological method both through misapplication and the permeation of society through a casual, popularized psychology (p. 259).

[7] Louf, 71.

[8] J. Laidlaw, "Heart," *Hastings Dictionary of the Bible* (Edinburgh: T & T. Clark, 1899) 317.

[9] W. E., Vine, *A Comprehensive Dictionary of the Origin Greek Words with Their Precise Meanings for English Readers* (McLean VA: Macdonald Publishing Co.) 546-47.

[10] Andre Louf, *Teach Us To Pray* (Boston: Cowley Publications, 1992) 9.

[11] Henry David Thoreau, *Walden Pond I*, ed. C. Merton Babcock (White Plains NY: Peter Pauper Press Inc.) 12.

[12] Louf, *The Cistercian Way*, 77.

Suggested Readings

Louf, Andre. *Teach Us To Pray.* Boston: Cowley Publications, 1992. Guidance for Christians seeking to deepen the life of prayer.

Louf, Andre. *The Cistercian Way.* Kalamazoo MI: Cistercian Publications, 1989. A model of spiritual leadership based on "the Cistercian way." An accessible and refreshing alternative to the worn-out paradigms.

O'Connor, Flannery. *The Violent Bear It Away.* New Yor: Farrar, Straus, and Giroux, 1960. Refutes Descartes and gives commentary on holy baptism.

O'Connor, Flannery. *Wise Blood*. New York: Farrar, Straus, and Giroux, 1979. Probes the nature of ministry and dissects the many caricatures of Christian ministry that have grown since O'Connor's death (1964) into national media phenomena.

Contributors

Gloria Armstrong, M.A., M.Div., an ordained Southern Baptist minister, is a licensed marriage and family therapist currently serving as a counselor with New Horizons Mental Health Services in Columbus, Georgia. She previously worked as a counselor with the Pastoral Institute, also in Columbus. Rev. Armstrong is the author of several articles on grief and trauma work as they relate to pastoral-clinical practice.

Edwin Chase, D.Min., a certified pastoral counselor, is Director of the Family Institute at the Methodist Home for Children and Youth in Macon, Georgia, and the United Methodist Conference Pastoral Counselor for the South Georgia District. Previously, Dr. Chase served as Director of the Clergy Resource Center, which he founded in 1991 at the Pastoral Institute in Columbus, Georgia, and as a pastor.

James Johnson, D.Min, died of cancer following completion of his chapter written for this book. He was the longtime beloved pastor of First Presbyterian Church in Columbus Georgia, highly regarded for his down-to-earthness, biblical scholarship, and pastoral acumen. He taught briefly at Princeton Theological Seminary prior to his death. Jim is also known for "walking the first person through the doors of the Pastoral Institute" when it was founded in 1974.

Ron King, Ph.D., a licensed marriage and family therapist, is Executive Director/CEO of the Pastoral Institute in Columbus, Georgia. He is chairman of the board of the Columbus Chamber of Commerce and past president of the Downtown Columbus Rotary Club. Dr. King is a fellow in the American Association of Pastoral Counselors and is a clinical member and approved supervisor of the American Association of Marriage and Family Therapists.

Stephen Muse, Ph.D., senior pastoral psychotherapist and Director of Counselor Training at the Pastoral Institute in Columbus, Georgia, teaches part-time at Columbus State University and the U.S. Army Family Life Training program at Fort Benning and is adjunct faculty at Garrett Evangelical Seminary in Illinois. He has served in pastoral and counseling ministries of the Presbyterian and Greek Orthodox churches. Dr. Muse is editor of *The Pastoral Forum*, writer of a column for the *Columbus Ledger/Enquirer* focusing on spirituality and health, and author of numerous articles. He is a Diplomate in the American Association of Pastoral Counselors, an AAMF approved supervisor, and is licensed in the state of Georgia as a professional counselor and marriage and family therapist. Areas of specialty include trauma, marriage therapy, and working with clergy and other helping professionals in crisis.

Barrett Smith, D.Min., is Associate Director of the Turner Clergy Center of the Pastoral Institute in Columbus, Georgia. He is an ordained United Methodist minister and served several pastorates in the local church prior to joining the Pastoral Institute. Barrett has special expertise in the area of church conflict and has been involved in consultation services in a variety of denominations.

Jeffrey Wilson, M. Div., M.Litt., has served as pastor of Westminster Presbyterian Church in York, Pennsylvania, since 1983. He has been president of the county council of Harford County, Maryland, and for many years has written a weekly newspaper column. Reverend Wilson lives and works on a family farm in Street, Maryland.

Appendix

The D. A. and Elizabeth Turner Clergy Center of the Pastoral Institute, Incorporated, is dedicated to supporting clergy, their families, and congregations by providing a wide array of clinical, educational, and consultative programs.

Through the *Clergy Care Program*, ministers from anywhere in the United States may have up to six complimentary individual counseling sessions or twelve for a couple or family. Crisis intervention is available through the *Clergy-in-Crisis Program*, which provides a week of intensive counseling, spiritual direction, and professional consultation in a tranquil and relaxing retreat setting where emotional, relational, and spiritual health can be restored.

The *Clergy Help Line* (1-800-649-6446) is available for ministers to call for brief consultation, crisis management, emotional support, referral, and resources.

Regional lecture series and seminars are offered annually, featuring nationally prominent speakers and church leaders. In conjunction with the *Counselor Training Program*, various workshops and professional training opportunities provide specialized instruction for clergy in the ministry of pastoral care and counseling.

A *pulpit supply ministry* enlists carefully selected, highly-qualified clergy for those times when ministers need to be away from the pulpit. As an important way of combating clergy isolation, the staff of Turner Clergy Center also conduct a *weekly support group* for area ministers.

Through its *Congregational Assistance Program* and *Ministerial Assistance Program*, the Center maintains formal, contractual relationships with denominational bodies and local congregations. The Congregational Assistance Program is an exciting ministry that furnishes counseling services, life enrichment education, and professional development opportunities for members of congregations through a contractual relationship with the Pastoral Institute. The Ministry Assistance Program is a joint ministry between a denominational body and the Pastoral Institute that provides counseling services and clergy crisis intervention for ministers and their families to assist clergy in coping with the challenges and demands of parish life and work.

The Turner Clergy Center also provides *vocational counseling* to ministers who may need career assessment or reevaluation at critical points along their career path. For those who are in the initial phases of the ordination process, we provide the full range of testing apparatuses required by most mainline denominations as well as a clinical evaluation designed to help determine a candidate's fitness for ministry.

The Turner Clergy Center expresses its commitment to continuing clergy and congregational support through its print and electronic publications and ongoing research projects aimed at better understanding the obstacles that impact clergy and congregational life. A free, biannual publication, *The Bridge*, addresses those issues most pressing for today's clergy while highlighting the programs and upcoming events of the Center. It includes book reviews; notices of seminars and workshops; important information about special programs available to congregations; and suggestions for personal, professional, and spiritual growth. With circulation now more than 6,000, *The Bridge* has become a vital link to clergy throughout the southeastern United States.

Staff regularly contribute articles to *The Pastoral Forum*, a journal published by the Pastoral Institute and dedicated to the advancement of the pastoral counseling movement. The Pastoral Forum seeks to explore the meaningful relationship between God and people and cultivate an ongoing dialogue between theology and psychology, faith and clinical practice. *Like A Tree Planted: A Minister's Guide to Resiliency* is an electronic publication posted on the Pastoral Institute web page that addresses and gives suggestions for coping with the many challenges that clergy face today.

For more information
<http://www.pastoralinstitute.org> [Turner Clergy Center icon]
<crcmail@pastoralinstitute.org>